A SENSE OF HISTORY

Medieval Realms
1066–1500

JAMES MASON

LONGMAN

Acknowledgements

We are grateful to the following for permission to reproduce photographs: Aerofilms Ltd, page 42 *below*; Ancient Art & Architecture Collection/©Ronald Sheridan, pages 33, 64, 101, 121; Keith Barley, page 66 *below left*; Bibliotheek de Rijksuniversiteit te Leiden, page 92; Bibliotheque de Rouen, page 50 *above* (Lauros-Giraudon); Bibliotheque Nationale, Paris, pages 57 *below right*, 117; Bibliotheque Royale de Belgique, Brussels, page 105; Bibliotheque Sainte-Geneviève, Paris, page 41 *above left*; Birmingham Museum & Art Gallery, page 124; Bodleian Library, Oxford, pages 12 *below*, 24 *below*, 25, 29 *above*, 49 *above left*, 55(2), 60 *right*, 69, 74, 102 *left*; Bridgeman Art Library, page 70; Brighton Reference Library, page 38; Bristol Record Office, page 52; British Library, pages 9 *below*, 22, 32, 37, 39, 40, 41 *above right*, 41 *below*, 43, 44, 49 *below*, 51, 53 *below*, 56(2), 57 *above left*, 57 *above right*, 61, 68, 72, 89, 91, 93 *above right*, 96(3), 97 *below right*, 98(2), 106 *below left*, 111, 114, 115; British Museum, London, page 95; Cambridge University Library, page 60 *below left*; E.T. Archive, pages 24 *above left*, 24 *above right*, 73; Mary Evans Picture Library, page 66 *above*; Fotografie della Societa Scala, Firenze, pages 60 *above left*, 62 (Prato Galleria, Comunale); Paul Gulson, page 127 *left*; © Sonia Halliday Photographs, page 93 *below*; © Michael Holford, pages 5, 8, 10, 12 *above*, 13, 14, 15, 17(2), 18, 65, 112; H.P. Kraus, Rare Books & Medieval Manuscripts, New York, page 104 *below right*; Lambeth Palace Library, page 9 *above left*; Alfred Lammer, pages 66 *below right*, 67 *below*; Macdonald/Aldus Archive, page 123 *above right*; Mansell Collection, pages 50 *below*, 79, 100, 106 *above*, 106 *below right*; Musee de l'Assistance Publique, Paris, page 75; National Portrait Gallery, London, pages 122(3), 123 *above left*, 123 *below left*, 123 *below centre*, 123 *below right*; National Trust Photographic Library, page 126 *below* (Brian Lawrence); Osterreichische Nationalbibliothek, Vienna, page 104 *above left*; Picturepoint, page 7; The Pierpont Morgan Library, New York, pages 9 *above right* (M708 front cover), 94, 97 *above* (M638 f.10v), 99 (M638 f.23); Public Record Office, London, pages 28 *right*, 29 *below*, 87; Royal Commission on the Historical Monuments of England, pages 57 *below left*, 67 *above*; Windsor Castle, Royal Library © 1990 Her Majesty The Queen, page 36; St Bride's Printing Library, London, page 118(3); Walter Scott (Bradford), page 93 *above left*; Scottish Record Office, Edinburgh, page 88 *above*; Telegraph Colour Library, page 4; Topham, page 35; The Master & Fellows of Trinity College Library, Cambridge, page 104 *below left*; The Board of Trinity College Library, Dublin, page 53 *above*; Universitatsbibliothek, Heidelberg, page 49 *above right*; Walters Art Gallery, Baltimore, USA, page 48; The Warburg Institute, London, page 28 *left*; Weidenfeld & Nicolson Archives, page 120 *right*; Woodmansterne Ltd, pages 20 (Jeremy Marks), 30, 42 *above*, 85, 88 *below*, 126 *above*, 126 *centre*, 127 *right*. We are unable to trace the following copyright holders and would be grateful for information that would enable us to do so, pages 77, 78, 97 *below left*. Cover: Portrait of Richard II, Collection Westminster Abbey © Michael Holford.

Addison Wesley Longman Limited
*Edinburgh Gate, Harlow, Essex, CM20 2JE, England
and Associated Companies throughout the World*

© Longman Group UK Limited 1991

First published 1991
Sixth impression 1996
ISBN 0 582 207355

*Typeset in Monotype Lasercomp 12/14pt Photina
Printed in China*
GCC/06

Designed by Michael Harris
Illustrated by Michael A. Hill and Oxford Illustrators Limited

Contents

1
The Norman Conquest

A sign in the sky

In 1066 a strange sight appeared in the night sky. A monk who saw it wrote:

SOURCE 1

Over all England there was seen a sign in the skies such as had never been seen before. Some said it was the star 'comet' which some call the star with hair; and it first appeared on 24 April and it shone all the week.

Anglo-Saxon Chronicle, 1066

SOURCE 2

i **Halley's Comet** In 1682 an astronomer called Edmund Halley worked out that this comet goes round the Sun once every seventy-six years. Halley's comet last appeared in 1986. It will come back again in 2061.

This is what people saw that week. Astronomers call it **Halley's Comet**. It is a ball of ice and dust that orbits the Sun. When it gets near the Sun it heats up so that gas and dust make a bright ring round its centre and then stream off behind like a tail.

Nobody knew what comets were in 1066, so everyone was afraid. People said that it must be a sign from God that terrible things were going to happen.

SOURCE 3

England and Normandy in 1066.

Terrible things did happen that year. In September, William, Duke of Normandy, crossed the Channel from France and invaded England with a great army. Harold, King of the English, who had just defeated a Danish invasion in the north at Stamford Bridge marched his army to meet the Normans just outside Hastings on the Sussex coast.

At the Battle of Hastings the Normans defeated the English and killed Harold. Then they marched to London and crowned William king instead.

This invasion and the fighting that followed, in which the Normans took control of England, are called the 'Norman Conquest'. Duke William, who became William, King of the English, is remembered as 'William the Conqueror'.

Some years after the Battle of Hastings William's brother, Odo, who was Bishop of Bayeux in Normandy, ordered needle workers to make pictures on cloth to tell the story of the battle and the events that led up to it. Today, we call this piece of needlework the Bayeux Tapestry.

SOURCE 4

This is how the Bayeux Tapestry shows the comet. You can see people pointing at it and someone giving a message to Harold. Find the boats in the bottom line of the tapestry below Harold. What do you think the message might be about?

- What were the English like in 1066?
- Who were the Normans? Where had they come from and what were they like?
- Why did a Norman, Duke William, want to conquer the English?
- How did the Normans manage to conquer the English?
- Did England stay the same with the Normans in charge?

The rest of Part 1 will help you to work out the answers to these questions for yourself.

> **ⓘ Anglo-Saxon Chronicle**
> Sometime around 891, King Alfred of Wessex ordered records to be collected about the history of the English from the time of the earliest Anglo-Saxon settlements. Monks wrote a list of events saying what happened, in what order, each year. The Chronicle was then sent to various monasteries – including Abingdon, Worcester and Peterborough – where monks kept it up to date. As a result, several versions have survived, though they all tell much the same story. The Peterborough Chronicle went on the longest, finishing in 1154.

England and the English

The Kingdom of England and the British Isles

SOURCE 5

The British Isles in 1066.

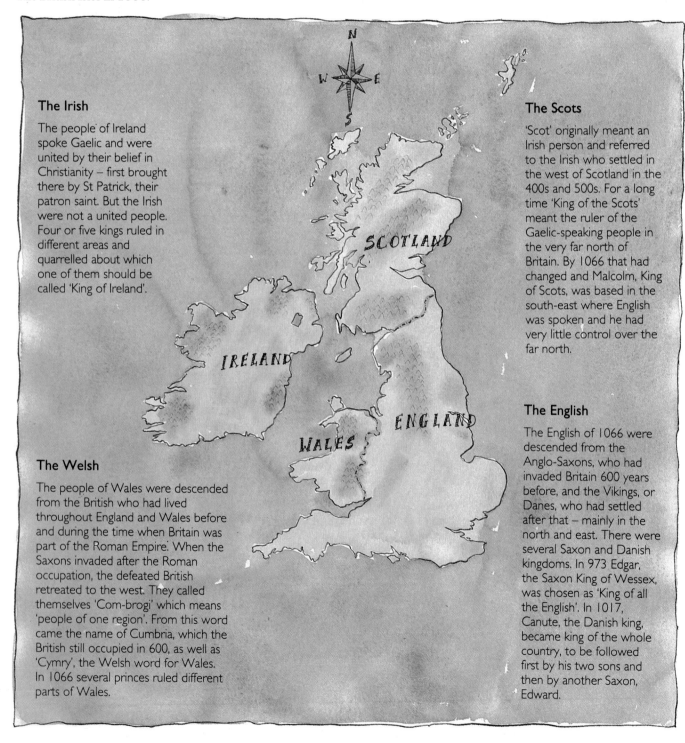

The Irish

The people of Ireland spoke Gaelic and were united by their belief in Christianity – first brought there by St Patrick, their patron saint. But the Irish were not a united people. Four or five kings ruled in different areas and quarrelled about which one of them should be called 'King of Ireland'.

The Scots

'Scot' originally meant an Irish person and referred to the Irish who settled in the west of Scotland in the 400s and 500s. For a long time 'King of the Scots' meant the ruler of the Gaelic-speaking people in the very far north of Britain. By 1066 that had changed and Malcolm, King of Scots, was based in the south-east where English was spoken and he had very little control over the far north.

The Welsh

The people of Wales were descended from the British who had lived throughout England and Wales before and during the time when Britain was part of the Roman Empire. When the Saxons invaded after the Roman occupation, the defeated British retreated to the west. They called themselves 'Com-brogi' which means 'people of one region'. From this word came the name of Cumbria, which the British still occupied in 600, as well as 'Cymry', the Welsh word for Wales. In 1066 several princes ruled different parts of Wales.

The English

The English of 1066 were descended from the Anglo-Saxons, who had invaded Britain 600 years before, and the Vikings, or Danes, who had settled after that – mainly in the north and east. There were several Saxon and Danish kingdoms. In 973 Edgar, the Saxon King of Wessex, was chosen as 'King of all the English'. In 1017, Canute, the Danish king, became king of the whole country, to be followed first by his two sons and then by another Saxon, Edward.

i Aelfric was famous as a teacher and wrote several books, some in English and some in Latin. Around 1005 he wrote his Colloquy in Latin, a book of conversations between a teacher and his pupil on one side and people with different jobs, on the other. This is full of Aelfric's thoughts on what life was like for different sorts of people at this time.

The English people

Around the year 1005 a monk called **Aelfric** wrote that the king of the English depended on three groups to support him – 'labourers, priests and warriors'. This is what he said about them:

SOURCE 6

> **Labourers** *are they who provide us with food, ploughmen and husbandmen [farmers] devoted to that alone.*
> **Priests** *are they who pray for us to God and promote Christianity among Christian peoples in the service of God, as spiritual work devoted to that alone for the benefit of us all.*
> **Warriors** *are they who guard our boroughs [towns] and also our land, fighting with weapons against the oncoming army.*
>
> Aelfric, *Colloquy*, 1005

SOURCE 7

At work in the fields. Drawn by a monk in about 1000. What job can you see being done? What information about the English in about 1000 can you work out from this source?

The labourers

Most ordinary English people lived in villages in houses made of wood, clay and straw and made their living from farming. Some owned their house and some land, but many owned nothing and were slaves, or serfs, who had to work for someone else. Even free people had someone who they called their 'lord'. They had to promise to fight for their lord when needed. If they lived on his estate they had to work for him for several days a week in return for the land that they farmed for themselves.

activity

What does source 6 tell you about England around 1005?
1a Copy this box and put a tick in the column that you think is right for each statement in the left-hand column.
b How could you find out if the things you have ticked as 'possibly true' are true or not?
2 Aelfric was a Christian monk. What difference do you think that made to what he wrote?
3 Aelfric was describing what he thought were the most important groups of people in England in 1005. What do you think are the most important groups today?

	True	Possibly true	False
Everyone in England was a Christian			
Christianity was important			
Everyone in England grew food			
The English were fighting a war			
The English had enemies who often attacked them			
There were towns in England			
There were a lot of towns in England			

The priests

England had been Christian for hundreds of years by 1066.

SOURCE 8

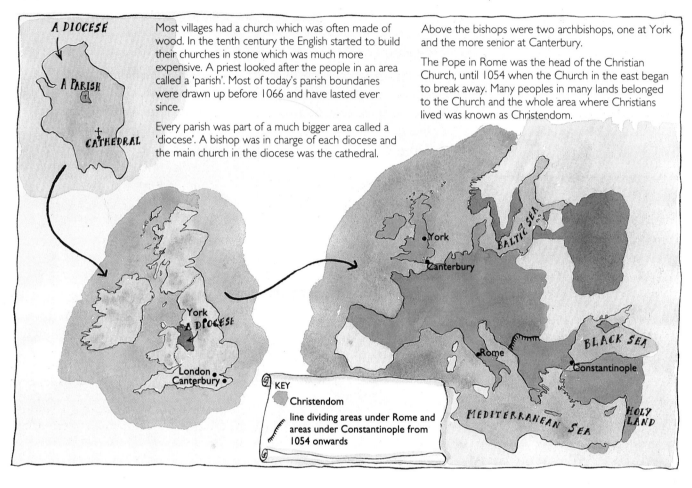

Most villages had a church which was often made of wood. In the tenth century the English started to build their churches in stone which was much more expensive. A priest looked after the people in an area called a 'parish'. Most of today's parish boundaries were drawn up before 1066 and have lasted ever since.

Every parish was part of a much bigger area called a 'diocese'. A bishop was in charge of each diocese and the main church in the diocese was the cathedral.

Above the bishops were two archbishops, one at York and the more senior at Canterbury.

The Pope in Rome was the head of the Christian Church, until 1054 when the Church in the east began to break away. Many peoples in many lands belonged to the Church and the whole area where Christians lived was known as Christendom.

KEY

Christendom

line dividing areas under Rome and areas under Constantinople from 1054 onwards

SOURCE 9

All Saints' Church, Earls Barton. The tower was built in the tenth century. The battlements at the top were added later.

activity

I What does source 9 tell you about the skills of English builders?

A great many English men and women chose to become monks and nuns. They lived in monasteries and nunneries which were places where they were cut off from other people and where they spent their lives worshipping God. Monks and nuns learnt to read and write in both Latin and English. They wrote, illustrated and copied books for other people.

SOURCE 10

A monk drew this picture in the tenth century. It shows a seventh-century monk called Adhelm giving the nuns of Barking Abbey a book that he had written for them in Latin. Adhelm wrote it all out by hand. If the nuns needed more copies they had to copy it out themselves.

SOURCE 11

English monks made this cover for a bible in around 1060. Among the materials used by the monks are gold, precious stones and pearls. The bottom half shows Christ on the Cross, with His mother, the Virgin Mary, and St John. The top half shows Christ ruling in Heaven surrounded by angels.

activity

2 Many of sources 1–12 show the work of monks and nuns. Which ones are they?
3 What does source 11 tell you about the craftsmanship and artistic skills of the monks?
4 The word 'rich' can mean having things of value which are not just worth money. Does source 11 suggest that England was **a** wealthy, and **b** rich in other ways?

The warriors

The English called the chief landowners 'eorls' (earls) and 'thegns' (thanes). The thanes had to serve the king in war and they had to make sure that the defences and fortifications of the towns were in good repair. Fortified towns were called 'boroughs'. If an enemy attacked the people living in the countryside around they would take refuge in the borough. The borough was also a place where they could hold a market in safety.

SOURCE 12

A thane. Drawn by a monk in the eleventh century.

activity

5 What are the differences between the thane's clothes (source 12), those of the labourer (source 7) and the monk's and nuns' clothes (source 10)? Who do you think was the best dressed? Who was the worst?

The king

When an English king was crowned, he made three promises: to make good laws; to protect the weak and to punish people who did wrong. Look at source 13. Find the things that Harold has been given to show he is king:

- the crown
- the sceptre (the rod or wand)
- the orb (the globe with a cross on the top)
- the sword of state (this stands for justice)

activity

I Look at source 13. Find the archbishop who has crowned Harold. He has also just anointed him with oil.
a Why do you think the Church thought it was important for an archbishop to crown and anoint the king?
b Why do you think the king thought it was a good idea to be crowned and anointed by an archbishop?

By the tenth century, English kings had divided England into 'shires', later called counties (see source 14). Each shire had a court which had to meet twice a year. The person who summoned the court in the name of the king was called the 'shire-reeve', or sheriff. Boroughs were royal towns and the king was most powerful where there were boroughs.

activity

Look at source 14.
2a How many boroughs are marked?
b Where are the boroughs packed closest together and where are there no boroughs or very few?
3a Copy the map and shade in the area where you think the king was most powerful.
b Is it true to say that the king's power was equally strong all over England?

SOURCE 13

King Harold's coronation. From the Bayeux Tapestry.

SOURCE 14

English shires and boroughs.

The Normans

Who were they?

'Norman' means 'Northman'. The Normans took their name from the Viking pirates who had invaded both England and France in the ninth century.

After many battles the English had to accept that the Vikings were settled for good in northern England. In France, Charles, King of the Franks, faced the same problem. In 911 he decided to hand over the northern part of his lands to the Viking leader, Rollo. Rollo became the first duke of 'Northmannia', 'the land of the Northmen' – Normandy.

The Viking chiefs became the new owners of the land in Normandy, but the ordinary French people who lived there stayed on. Vikings and French married each other so that by 1066 the Normans were as much French as Viking.

What were they like?

The Normans liked to think of themselves as special, and different from other French people. They particularly enjoyed this story about what happened when King Charles gave Normandy to Rollo:

SOURCE 15

The Frankish bishops said, 'Anyone who received such a gift ought to bend down and kiss the King's foot.' But Rollo said, 'Never will I bend my knees to anyone, nor will I kiss anyone's foot.' But the Franks insisted, so Rollo ordered a certain soldier to kiss the King's foot. The soldier immediately took hold of the King's foot, lifted it up to his mouth and kissed it without kneeling down, so that the King was toppled over backwards.

Dudo, *The Manners and Deeds of the First Dukes of Normandy*, written about 1020

This is what a monk writing in England had to say about the Normans a hundred years later:

SOURCE 16

In 1066 the Normans, as they are now, were very fussy about their clothes and enjoyed their food, but they were not greedy. They are so used to war that they can hardly live without it.

William of Malmesbury, *Deeds of the Kings of the English*, 1125

---

activity

4 Which of these words do you think best describes the Normans in the story in source 15:

friendly	rude
strong	timid
stupid	brave
angry	arrogant
polite	obedient
proud	

5 Why might this story please the Normans a hundred years after it happened? Do you think it was likely to be a true story?

---

i William of Malmesbury was half English and half Norman. He was brought up in Malmesbury Abbey where he became a monk. He collected information about the history of the English. He travelled widely in England.

SOURCE 17

Loading ships ready for their invasion of England. From the Bayeux Tapestry.
Find:
- suits of armour. How heavy are they? How can you tell?
- helmets, swords, spears and a battle-axe
- wooden casks of wine
- a cart. What is on it? How well have the soldiers loaded it?

activity

Ia What does source 17 tell you about the way the Normans prepared to invade England?
b What did they think was important?

The Bayeux Tapestry tells us a lot about the Normans and war. Source 17 shows some of their preparations for invading England.

When the Normans' ancestors, the Vikings, first invaded France, they robbed its Christian churches and monasteries. But, once they had settled there, they became Christian. By 1000 there were five monasteries in Normandy. By 1066 there were more than thirty. Source 18 shows one of four big churches the Normans built in 1066.

activity

Look at source 18.
2 What does it tell you about the skills of Norman builders?
3 Do you think it costs a lot to build a church such as Jumièges? What are your reasons?
4 Do you think that source 18 and the information in the text show that religion was important to the Normans? Why?

SOURCE 18

The now ruined Norman church of Notre Dame (Our Lady) at Jumièges. It was finished in 1067.
- What materials have the Normans used?
- Make drawings of the windows and door. The Normans invented these shapes. They help to give the building its special look or 'Norman style'.

assignments

I What kinds of people were the Normans who invaded England in 1066? Make a list of the words that you think describe the Normans best and write a few sentences to explain why you have chosen each word.

2 Sources 9 and 18 are modern photographs of buildings that have survived for about a thousand years. How can buildings tell us about what was important to people in the past?

Why did Duke William invade England?

King Edward dies

When the comet appeared over England in April 1066, Harold had been king for only three months. King Edward had died the previous January leaving no child to succeed him. Shortly before he died he named Harold Godwinson, one of the chief earls, as his successor.

The other earls wanted to avoid a fight for the crown so they quickly met and accepted Harold as their king. He was already the most powerful among them and he was a good soldier. They hoped he would keep the peace.

They buried Edward in London, in Westminster Abbey which had only just been built. They crowned Harold the same day. 'Earl Harold was now consecrated king,' wrote the author of the *Anglo-Saxon Chronicle*, 'and he met little quiet in it as long as he ruled the realm [kingdom].'

SOURCE 19

The Bayeux Tapestry shows the body of King Edward being carried to Westminster Abbey. You can see a builder fixing on the last weather cock as the funeral procession arrives.

Who should be king?

Two other rulers thought they had a claim to the English crown. One was Harald Hardraada, King of Norway. The other was Duke William of Normandy.

William said that Edward, whose mother had been a Norman, had named him as the next king of England many years before. He said that Harold himself had been to Normandy in 1064 and had sworn a solemn oath to support William's claim. Now Harold had broken his promise.

William called his knights together and persuaded them to help him to punish Harold and win the crown that he said was his. He ordered them to meet him at the coast with their soldiers ready for the sea-crossing to England.

Viewpoints

SOURCE 20

Edward, king of the English, being without an heir, sent Robert, Archbishop of Canterbury, to the duke with a message appointing the duke as heir to the kingdom which God had entrusted to him.

William of Jumièges, *Deeds of the Norman Dukes*, 1070

SOURCE 21

activity

1 Look at sources 20 and 21 which show what the Normans said happened before King Edward died. How do they support William's claim that Edward promised he would become the next king of England?

The Bayeux Tapestry shows Harold making an oath to William.

SOURCE 22

Edward, in bed, speaks to his most trusted followers. Harold is shown at the front. From the Bayeux Tapestry.

Normanay. Later he became a priest and was made chaplain to Duke William. He did not go with the duke on his expedition to England; but he was in a good position to find out what happened from those who did.

SOURCE 23

A messenger from Harold is speaking to William just before the battle of Hastings:

'He certainly remembers that King Edward long ago decided that you would be his heir, and that he himself in Normandy gave surety to you concerning that succession. Nevertheless, he knows that this kingdom is his by right, as granted to him by gift of that same king his lord on his deathbed.'

William of Poitiers, *The Deeds of William, Duke of the Normans and King of the English*, written about 1071

SOURCE 24

There came the unwelcome report that the land of England had lost its king, and that Harold had been crowned in his stead. This unfeeling Englishman did not wait for the public choice, but breaking his oath, and with the support of a few discontented friends, he seized the throne of the best of kings on the very day of his funeral, and when all the people were bewailing their loss.

SOURCE 25

The next day Edward was buried in kingly style amid the bitter lamentations of all present. After his burial the under-king Harold, son of Godwine, whom the king had nominated as his successor, was chosen king by the chief magnates of all England; and on the same day Harold was crowned with great ceremony.

activity

2 Look at sources 22 and 23.
a How do they support Harold's claim that Edward made him his successor at the last moment?
b Are they Norman or English sources?
c Does that make Harold's argument stronger or weaker? Why?
3 Look at sources 24 and 25. One was written by a Norman and one by an Englishman.
a Which is which? How can you tell?
b Why do you think the two sources report the same events in such different ways?
4 Sources 20, 21 and 24 all support William's claim to the throne of England. What difference would it make if sources 22, 23 and 25 did not exist?

The Battle of Hastings

Invaders

When King Harold heard that Duke William was preparing to invade, he told his soldiers to guard the south coast from Sandwich in Kent right round to the Isle of Wight. All that summer they watched and waited. In September the soldiers had to return home to bring in the harvest. Harold went back to London. Just as he arrived a messenger brought news. There had been an invasion. Harold must come quickly.

But the invasion was in the north, not the south. Harald Hardraada, King of Norway, had landed. He was supported by Harold's younger brother, Tostig. Harold marched north as fast as he could. On 25 September he caught the invaders by surprise beyond York at Stamford Bridge. A fierce battle raged and many were killed on both sides before the English won. Tostig died. So did Harald Hardraada.

On 27 September William of Normandy's soldiers boarded 3,000 ships and that night they sailed for England. The next morning they landed at Pevensey in Sussex. As soon as Harold heard the news he rushed south again. Some of his bravest fighters had died at Stamford Bridge and he reached Sussex with his soldiers tired from the march. Even so he pushed on towards Hastings where William had made his camp. William moved out to meet him. He came upon Harold early in the morning of Saturday 14 October.

The battle

The most detailed account of the battle that followed comes from William of Poitiers. Duke William, he tells us, put his archers in the front, infantry in armour behind them and knights on horses at the back. The English took up their position on a hill where they kept close together to make a solid wall of shields which the Normans could not get through.

Suddenly part of the Norman army broke and ran away from the English. The word went round that William had been killed and part of his army started to retreat:

SOURCE 26

The duke pushed himself in front of those who were running away, shouting at them and threatening them with his spear. He stopped their retreat, took off his helmet, and standing before them bareheaded he cried 'Look at me well. I am still alive and by the grace of God I shall yet prove the victor . . .' With these words he restored their courage and . . . the Normans then surrounded several thousands of their pursuers and rapidly cut them down so that not one escaped.

William of Poitiers, *The Deeds of William*, 1071

SOURCE 27

The Bayeux Tapestry shows the Anglo-Saxons defending their hill.

Once again the Normans attacked the shield-wall but the English stood so tightly together that there was not even space for the dead to fall down. The Normans realised that they could not make any progress while the English were packed so closely together, so twice they pretended to retreat. The English followed but the Normans turned around and attacked them, and then returned to attack the English still on the hill.

SOURCE 28

This scene from the Bayeux Tapestry shows the height of the battle with both men and horses killed.

SOURCE 29

This [English] army was still formidable [strong] and very difficult to overwhelm [defeat]. Indeed this was a battle of a new type: one side vigorously attacking; the other resisting as if rooted to the ground.

At last the English began to weary. Evening was now falling, they knew that their king with two of his brothers and many other great men had been killed. Those who remained were almost exhausted, and they realised that they could expect no more help.

They began to flee as swiftly as they could, some on foot, some along the roads, but most over the trackless country. The Normans eagerly carried on the pursuit, and striking the rebels in the back brought a happy end to this famous victory.

William of Poitiers, *The Deeds of William*, 1071

SOURCE 30

The Bayeux Tapestry shows the death of Harold. You can read the Latin 'Harold Rex interfectus est' which means, 'King Harold was killed'.

activity

Work in pairs.
1a Look at sources 27, 28, and 30. Make a list of all the ways in which the Norman and English armies were the same. Make another of all the ways in which they were different.
b William of Poitiers says the English were very difficult to beat. Why might he have wanted to say that? Do you think he was right? Give your reasons.

assignments

1a Make a list of all the reasons you can think of why the Normans won the battle of Hastings and put them under one of these headings.

Things that happened before the battle.
Things that happened during the battle.

b Now put the points under each heading in the order in which they happened.
c Which do you think were the two most important reasons under each heading? Underline them. Write a few sentences to say why you think this.

2 Now organise a class discussion about which were the most important reasons why the Normans won the battle. People who agree with each other get together beforehand to plan their arguments. See if you change your mind because of the discussion.

What did the Norman Conquest change?

What would the English do after the battle of Hastings? William waited to find out. Nothing happened. No messengers came, no offer of the crown.

After five days he made a move. The surviving English earls gathered in London to try to decide what to do. William did not make straight for London, but took a long route round, burning houses and taking food as he went.

SOURCE 31

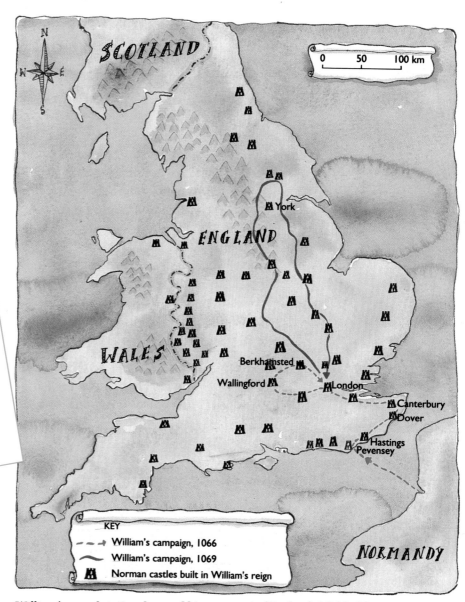

activity

2 Look at source 31. Why do you think William crossed the Thames at Wallingford instead of at London Bridge on his first march to London?

3 Look at sources 31 and 14 on page 10. Which parts of the country do you think William found it most difficult to control? Why?

KEY
- – – ➤ William's campaign, 1066
- ⎯⎯ William's campaign, 1069
- ⚔ Norman castles built in William's reign

William's march to London and his conquest of England, 1066–69.

activity

1 Read source 32.
a Why do you think William did this? What does it tell you about him?
b Do you think that the English expected their king to behave like this? Explain your reasons for your answer.
c Do you think what William did (i) made sense from his point of view, and (ii) was right? Explain your reasons.

At Berkhamsted he stopped. There the chief earls and bishops met him and swore to obey him. On Christmas Day, 1066, they crowned him King of the English in Westminster Abbey.

William of Normandy may have been crowned king of England, but that did not mean that everyone accepted him. It took him four more years of fighting before he had control of the whole country. The worst rebellion was in 1069 when two English earls, helped by a Danish fleet, captured York and killed many hundreds of Normans. William acted at once:

SOURCE 32

William fell on the English of Yorkshire like a lion out to kill. He ordered their houses, corn, tools and goods to be burnt and large herds of cattle and oxen to be butchered. Thousands of children, old people and young men and women died of hunger.

Orderic Vitalis, *History of the Church,* completed in 1141

SOURCE 33

A modern photograph of the castle that William built at York. The mound of earth, which the Normans called a motte, originally had a wooden tower on it. The stone tower was built later. A ditch went right around the motte and a wooden bridge would have connected the motte with the other side of the ditch. Who do you think would actually have done the digging to make a castle like this – English or Normans?

Castles

SOURCE 34

William went in the spring overseas to Normandy. And Bishop Odo and Earl William stayed behind in charge and built castles far and wide throughout the land, oppressing the wretched people, and things went continually from bad to worse.

Anglo-Saxon Chronicle, 1066–67

There were very few castles in England before the Normans came. Look at the map (source 31 on page 19). How many were there by the end of William's reign?

SOURCE 35

The fortifications called castles by the Normans were scarcely known in England and so the English – in spite of their courage and love of fighting – could put up only weak resistance to their enemies.

Orderic Vitalis, *History of the Church,* 1141

activity

2 Look at sources 31, 33 and 34. What was the use of a castle?
3 Do you think the Normans and the English felt differently about castles?
Use sources 33, 34 and 35 to say how they both felt.

The feudal system

After the last English rebellions in 1071 William started to take land away from the English earls and give it to the Normans. He wanted to punish the English landowners who had been disloyal and reward the Norman knights who had helped him. A knight who became one of the chief landowners was called a baron.

William gave the land to each baron in a special way shown in the diagram.

SOURCE 36

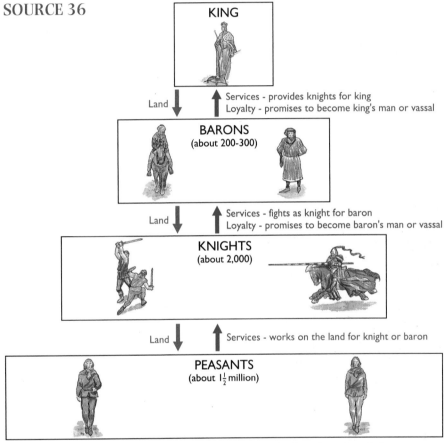

First the baron knelt down, put his hands between the king's and said, 'I promise to become your man, to hold these lands faithfully and perform my due service, preserving your earthly honour in all things.' Then the king said, 'I take you to be my man.' Then the baron stood up, placed one hand on the Bible and swore to be loyal to the king. This system went on right down to the holder of the smallest plot of land in every village. It is called the Feudal System. William used it to make sure that every single bit of land in England had been granted by the king and could be taken away by him too.

Domesday Book

In 1086 William decided that he needed to know exactly who owned what land and how much money they could give him. So he sent investigators to every district, or 'hundred', in every shire. The

Orderic Vitalis *was born in England in 1075. He had a Norman father and an English mother. When he was ten his father sent him to Normandy to become a monk. He lived in a Norman monastery for the rest of his life and there he wrote a book called* The History of the Church *which went right up to his own times.*

activity

4 When William gave land to a baron, the baron promised to perform his 'due service' in return. Look at source 36. What service did the baron have to give the king?

SOURCE 37

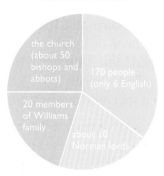

Who owned the land?

Total population of England: about 2 million
Total number of Normans in England: about 10,000

A chart showing some information from Domesday Book about England in 1086.

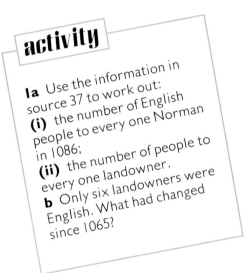

activity

1a Use the information in source 37 to work out:
(i) the number of English people to every one Norman in 1086;
(ii) the number of people to every one landowner.
b Only six landowners were English. What had changed since 1065?

activity

2 Look at source 38. Do you think the women are hunting for sport or for food?
3 What do you think ordinary people felt about the Forest Laws?

English named the book where they recorded their findings 'Domesday Book' because it reminded them of 'Doomsday', the Last Day of Judgement, when God would judge all living people and the dead.

He told them to bring people together from every village in the hundred and ask them a lot of questions such as who owns the land, how much of it can be ploughed, how much woodland is there, how much meadow, how much is it worth, how many freemen are there, how many unfree, how many animals of various sorts?

The forest laws

The English kings had set aside special places to hunt called Royal Forests. William decided to make them much bigger. He made laws to stop ordinary people hunting there and some people were turned out of their homes. His son, William Rufus, who succeeded him in 1087 as William II, did the same. By 1100 a quarter of the country was royal forest.

SOURCE 38

Hunting.

The Church

By 1090 only one out of sixteen bishops was English, the rest were Norman:

SOURCE 39

England has become the property of foreigners. At the present time there is no English earl, nor bishop, nor abbot.

William of Malmesbury, *Deeds of the Kings of the English*, 1135

activity

4 Look at source 39. Why do you think the king thought it was important to have Normans as bishops and abbots?

The English had built most of their churches and cathedrals in wood and only a few in stone. Which material cost the most do you think? The Normans did not like the way they looked. By 1200 nearly every English church and cathedral had been rebuilt in stone in the Norman style.

Language and names

The English language has a lot of words which come from French. For instance, police, burglary, evidence, arrest, court, goal and justice were all originally French words. What do they have in common?

English mostly borrowed French words to do with the law, government and architecture. It did not borrow any words to do with farming and fishing. How does that fit in with what you know about the Normans?

assignments

1a Here are three pairs of words which we use in English today. One of each pair was originally English and one was French:

English	French
Cow	Beef (Boeuf)
Pig	Pork (Porc)
Sheep	Mutton (Mouton)

The words in each pair refer to the same animal. But if you think about it carefully you will find that there is a difference in the way we use them. What is it? How does it fit in with what you know about the Normans and the English?

b Names like 'William', 'Richard' and 'Robert' are originally French not English. We can use the evidence of first names to find out about what the English thought of the Normans as time went on. This table shows the number of people who owned houses in Winchester and who also had French first names at four different dates:

1066	1110	1148	1207
29%	62%	66%	82%

(i) The number of Normans living in Winchester stayed roughly the same from just after 1066 onwards, so what do these figures tell you about the first names of English people?
(ii) What does this tell you about what English people thought of the Normans by the end of the twelfth century?

c Here are three things that changed in England after William became king: Landholders; Forest Laws; Names.
(i) Write two or three sentences about each change to say what happened.
(ii) Say which of these changes happened rapidly, that is within twenty years, and which took place over a long period of time.

2 Some of the things we say are facts and some are points of view. For example, if I say to you, 'All dogs are animals', I am stating a fact. But if I say, 'All dogs are a nuisance', I am not stating a fact, I am stating a point of view. You may not agree with my point of view and we could argue about which of us is right.

a Here are two more statements, this time about William the Conqueror: 'William I was king of England. He was a better king than Harold.' One is a fact and one is a point of view. This chart shows which is which. Copy it out.

Fact	Point of view
William was king of England.	He was a better king than Harold.

b Now look at source 34 on page 20. Some of its statements are facts and some are points of view. Decide which column on your chart is right for each statement and write it in.

2
The King Governs the Realm

King Henry's nightmare

Henry was the youngest son of William the Conqueror. He had become king in 1100 after his elder brother, William Rufus, had died in a hunting accident.

SOURCE 1

> *Henry was a good man and people were in great awe of him. No one dared injure another in his time. He made peace for man and beast.*
>
> *Anglo-Saxon Chronicle, 1137*

That is what was said about Henry I after his death in 1137. If it is right he must have been a strong and confident king. In many ways he was, but that does not mean that he had no worries.

The abbot of a French monastery reported that Henry was so frightened of plots that he kept changing the position of his bed and always had his sword and shield hung near to hand; and John of Worcester, an English monk, described Henry's nightmare in which all three orders of society – peasants (labourers), knights (warriors) and clergy (priests) – rose up in rebellion against him.

SOURCE 2

The knights.

The peasants.

The clergy.

You can see from the pictures that went with John's story how each group in turn came up to the bed of the sleeping king and threatened him with weapons as they complained that he asked for too many taxes.

1 What clues does source 1 give about the things ordinary people wanted the king to do?

2 What problems did Henry I have to cope with according to source 3?

3 How does source 3 help to explain John of Worcester's story (source 2)?

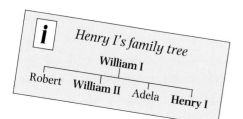

i Henry I's family tree

William I

Robert   William II   Adela   Henry I

SOURCE 3

All this year King Henry stayed in Normandy because of the war with the king of France and the count of Anjou and the count of Flanders. Because of these wars the king was very much distressed and lost a great deal both in money and also in land. But those who troubled him most were his own men, who frequently deserted and betrayed him and went over to his enemies and surrendered their castles to them so as to injure and betray the king. England paid dear for all this because of the various taxes, which never ceased in the course of all this year.

Anglo-Saxon Chronicle, 1117

The end of hopes and plans

On 26 November 1121 Henry I arrived back in England after a long visit to Normandy. That afternoon a messenger arrived at court with terrible news. It was so bad that no one dared to tell the king. When he did eventually hear it Henry fell to the floor in shock and had to be led away to his room.

Orderic Vitalis wrote down the story shortly after it happened. According to Orderic a sailor called Thomas asked Henry if his ship, the White Ship, could take the king and his followers back to England. Henry had already made his own arrangements but allowed his sons, William and Richard, to travel in the White Ship. In all there were about 300 passengers on board, mostly barons and their sons. Everybody got very drunk and they persuaded Thomas to try to overtake all the other ships.

SOURCE 4

Henry I sailing back to England from Normandy.

Disaster struck – the ship hit a rock. Orderic goes on to tell us:

SOURCE 5

Two planks were shattered by the crash and the ship, alas! filled and went down. At this fearful moment the passengers and crew raised cries of distress but their mouths were soon stopped by the swelling waves and all perished together, except two who seized hold of the yard from which the sail was set . . .

Thomas, the master of the vessel, managed to recover his senses after his first plunge into the sea and raising his head above the water he cried out, 'What has become of the king's son?' The two men clinging to the yard-arm replied that he and all the others had perished. 'Then,' said Thomas, 'it is misery for me to live any longer.' And he abandoned himself to his fate in utter despair, preferring to meet it at once rather than face the rage of the king or drag out his days in a dungeon . . .

Berold, who was the poorest man of all the company and wore sheep-skin clothing, was the only one out of so many who survived to see the dawn of another day.

Orderic Vitalis, *History of the Church*, 1141

William was Henry's oldest son. Henry planned that there should be no problems when William succeeded him:

SOURCE 6

When he was barely twelve years old, all the free men of England and Normandy . . . had to promise him loyalty . . . Louis, king of France, had, in return for William's loyalty agreed that he should be Duke of Normandy. In negotiating these matters King Henry spent four years . . .

William of Malmesbury, *The Deeds of the Kings of the English*, 1125

activity

Look at source 6.
I What had Henry done to make sure that:
a The barons would accept William?
b Other kings and princes would accept him?
2 What evidence is there that Henry had taken a lot of trouble over all this?
3 What problems did William's death give Henry?

Civil war

When Henry died in 1135 there were two competitors for the throne – his daughter, Matilda, and his nephew, Stephen. Henry had made all his barons swear to support Matilda. But some of them didn't like the idea of a woman as ruler; and others didn't like the fact that she was married to Geoffrey, the French count of Anjou, who would rule with her.

Stephen moved quickly and had himself crowned before Matilda could reach England. He then spent most of his reign fighting either Matilda or the barons who supported her. She was a tough opponent and at one point managed to capture Stephen and rule for four years, even though she was never crowned. Eventually it was agreed that Matilda would give up her claim as long as her son should succeed Stephen as King Henry II.

Stephen's reign was described like this:

SOURCE 7

The barons filled the country full of castles and held them against the king. They sorely [badly] burdened the unhappy people of the country with forced labour on the castles. And when they were built, they filled them with devils and wicked men . . .

They levied taxes on the villages every so often, and called it 'protection money'. When the wretched people had no more to give, they robbed and burned all the villages, so that you could easily go a whole day's journey and never find anyone occupying a village, nor land tilled [cultivated]. Corn was dear, and meat and butter and cheese, because there was none in the country.

Anglo-Saxon Chronicle, 1137

activity

Read source 7.
4 How did ordinary people suffer during the civil war between Stephen and Matilda?
5 Do you think Henry was right to worry about the succession?

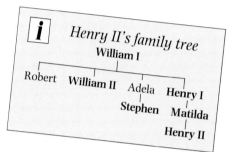

i **Henry II's family tree**
William I
Robert   William II   Adela   Henry I
Stephen   Matilda
Henry II

assignments

1 Choose a moment from the story of the sinking of the White Ship. Use sources 4 and 5, and any other information you can find to make either a model or a picture of that moment. Try to make everything as much as possible like it would have been in 1120. Make notes to show where you have had to make guesses and on what evidence you have based them.

2 John of Worcester drew three pictures to illustrate Henry I's fears. What other fears do you think Henry had? Draw a picture to illustrate each one.

3 The king normally controlled the barons. In the civil war the barons had a great deal more freedom. Do you think the barons felt the same about the civil war as the ordinary people? Why?

4 How important was it to have a strong king at this time? Give your reasons. Use what you have learnt from pages 24–27.

How Henry II governed

The headquarters of Henry II's government was at his Palace of Westminster in London. But he spent very little time there. Often he was not even in England.

He had an enormous kingdom to govern. In a reign of 32 years he crossed the English Channel 28 times and the Irish Sea twice; and he spent Christmas in 24 different places.

Wherever he went, even abroad, the members of his **Royal Household** went with him; but his Justiciar and his officials at **Westminster** and in the **Shires** always stayed in England to carry on the business of government for him.

'If the king has said he will remain in a place for a day – and particularly if he has announced his intention publicly by the mouth of a herald – he is sure to upset all the arrangements by departing early in the morning. And you then see men dashing around as if they were mad, beating packhorses, running carts into one another – in short, giving a lively imitation of Hell. If, on the other hand, the king orders an early start, he is sure to change his mind, and you can take it for granted that he will sleep until midday. Then you will see the packhorses loaded and waiting, the carts prepared, the courtiers dozing, traders fretting, and everyone grumbling. People go to ask the maids and doorkeepers what the king's plans are, for they are the only ones likely to know the secrets of the court.'

From a private letter written by Peter of Blois, Henry II's secretary.

THE ROYAL HOUSEHOLD
The Royal Household provided all the king's personal day to day needs and helped him govern. It was divided into four departments:

Hall	Constabulary	Chamber	Chancery
• bakers, butchers, cooks, butlers, cupbearers etc.	• marshals, huntsmen, stable boys, falconers, archers etc.	• tailors, water carriers, clothes washers, servants etc.	• chaplain, priests, clerks.
• provided, prepared and served food and drink for the court (200 – 300 people) every day.	• organised king's journeys and lodging, hunting and royal ceremonies. Protected king. Looked after royal horses, hounds, hawks and falcons.	• looked after the king's portable bed, his clothes, jewels and money.	• looked after portable chapel, held services, wrote out king's letters, charters and orders.
• run by the **Steward** (also in charge of provisions for the army in wartime).	• run by the **Marshal** (also in charge of all transport in wartime) and the **Constable** (also in charge of the army in wartime).	• run by the **Chamberlain** (also in charge of receiving newly minted coins and paying king's bills).	• run by the **Chancellor** who was in charge of the **Great Seal**.

Henry II's Great Seal. The seal was stamped onto sealing wax to make this picture which stood for the king's signature on his letters and orders.

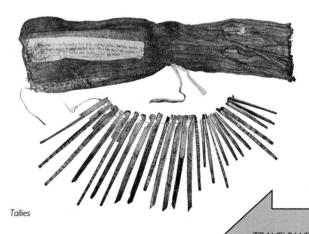

Tallies

TRAVELS WITH THE KING

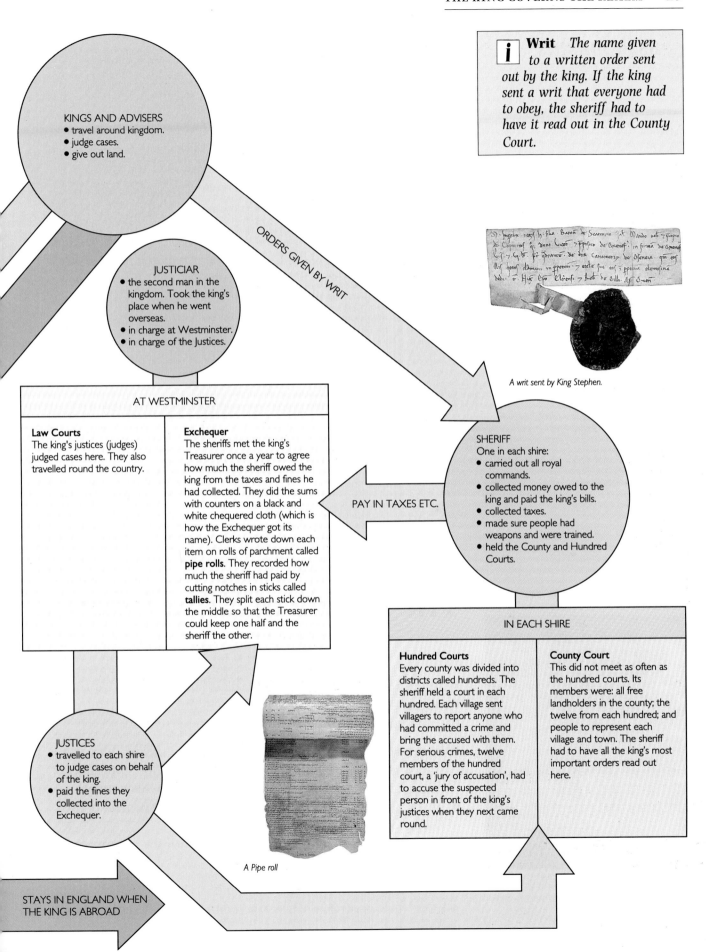

KINGS AND ADVISERS
- travel around kingdom.
- judge cases.
- give out land.

ORDERS GIVEN BY WRIT

JUSTICIAR
- the second man in the kingdom. Took the king's place when he went overseas.
- in charge at Westminster.
- in charge of the Justices.

i Writ *The name given to a written order sent out by the king. If the king sent a writ that everyone had to obey, the sheriff had to have it read out in the County Court.*

A writ sent by King Stephen.

AT WESTMINSTER

Law Courts
The king's justices (judges) judged cases here. They also travelled round the country.

Exchequer
The sheriffs met the king's Treasurer once a year to agree how much the sheriff owed the king from the taxes and fines he had collected. They did the sums with counters on a black and white chequered cloth (which is how the Exchequer got its name). Clerks wrote down each item on rolls of parchment called **pipe rolls**. They recorded how much the sheriff had paid by cutting notches in sticks called **tallies**. They split each stick down the middle so that the Treasurer could keep one half and the sheriff the other.

PAY IN TAXES ETC.

SHERIFF
One in each shire:
- carried out all royal commands.
- collected money owed to the king and paid the king's bills.
- collected taxes.
- made sure people had weapons and were trained.
- held the County and Hundred Courts.

IN EACH SHIRE

Hundred Courts
Every county was divided into districts called hundreds. The sheriff held a court in each hundred. Each village sent villagers to report anyone who had committed a crime and bring the accused with them. For serious crimes, twelve members of the hundred court, a 'jury of accusation', had to accuse the suspected person in front of the king's justices when they next came round.

County Court
This did not meet as often as the hundred courts. Its members were: all free landholders in the county; the twelve from each hundred; and people to represent each village and town. The sheriff had to have all the king's most important orders read out here.

JUSTICES
- travelled to each shire to judge cases on behalf of the king.
- paid the fines they collected into the Exchequer.

A Pipe roll

STAYS IN ENGLAND WHEN THE KING IS ABROAD

assignments

Here is the story of a boy called William Skywe:

SOURCE 8

Robert Badding, in climbing up a hayrick ... fell from the rick so that he broke his neck. John, William Skywe and Walter Stormy were ... present. William, accused of the death of Robert, ... denies it ... The jurors say he is guilty ... they say that Robert fell from the rick onto William and William, startled by this, struck Robert twice on the head with his staff [stick] so that it killed him. But they said that William did not do this in felony [serious crime] but rather out of witlessness because he is under age being 12 years old. So ... William will be taken into custody [imprisoned] and this case be told the king ...

From the Crown Pleas (cases heard by king's justices), Startley Hundred, Wiltshire, 1249

I The justices decided that 'this case be told the king' because only the king could pardon someone found guilty of causing another's death. Imagine you are King Henry III. What do you think the arguments were **a** against and **b** in favour of pardoning William?
2 Does this story of one boy help us to understand how the king's justice worked?

SOURCE 9

The head of the effigy of King John from his tomb in Worcester Cathedral. It was made about twenty years after his death.

The puzzle of King John

King John ruled from 1199 till his death in 1216. He was the youngest son of Henry II and succeeded his brother, Richard I. People remember John for three things in particular:

* he quarrelled with the Pope who excommunicated him as a punishment in 1209. That meant that the Pope stopped John being a member of the church until he said he was sorry
* he lost a war with the French king and so lost control of the Duchy of Normandy in 1214
* in 1215 he made a famous agreement with the barons which we call Magna Carta

The puzzle about King John is that both in the Middle Ages and in modern times historians have had completely different opinions about him:

i Relic An object such as a bit of clothing, a bone, hair or a personal possession that belonged to a holy person who is dead. In the Middle Ages people believed that relics had special powers and used them as charms.

activity

1 Look at sources 10–13.
a Which sources were written when John was alive or just after his death and which were written some time after his death?
b Which sources are very hostile to John and which give a more balanced view?
c How have historians' opinions about King John changed since 1200?
2 Look at sources 10 and 11. Make a list of the different points of view that these writers hold about King John.
3 Look at sources 12 and 13.
a Make a list of the different points of view that these two historians hold about King John.
b Which historian used source 10 and which used source 11?
4a Look at source 14. How does W. L. Warren show there is something wrong with Roger of Wendover's story?
b What does that tell you about sources 10 and 13?

SOURCE 10

*Foul as it is, Hell itself is defiled [polluted] by the fouler presence of King John . . . His punishments were refinements of cruelty – starvation of children, the crushing of old men under copes [long pieces] of lead . . . He scoffed [laughed] at priests and turned his back on the mass, even amidst the solemnities of his coronation, but he never stirred on a journey without hanging **relics** round his neck.*

J.R. Green, *Short History of the English People*, 1875

SOURCE 11

He was a great prince but hardly a happy one, and he experienced the ups and downs of fortune. He would have thought himself as happy and successful as he could have wished, had he not lost his continental possessions and suffered the Church's curse [excommunication].

Barnwell Chronicle, late 1220's

SOURCE 12

John sat as a judge. His lively mind and keen intelligence played upon the cases brought before him . . . No king of England was ever so unlucky . . . From the moment when France came into the strong hands of Philip II his conquest of Normandy was only a matter of time . . .

D.M. Stenton, *English Society in the Early Middle Ages*, 1951

SOURCE 13

John was a tyrant not a king, a destroyer instead of a governor, crushing his own people and favouring aliens [foreigners], a lion to his own people but a lamb to foreigners and rebels. He had lost the duchy of Normandy and many other territories though sloth [extreme laziness]. As for Christianity he was unstable and unfaithful . . . Foul as it is, Hell itself is defiled by the fouler presence of King John.

Matthew Paris, *Greater Chronicle*, 1235

Matthew Paris based what he said about John on another book, *The Flowers of History* by **Roger of Wendover**. Matthew took over from Roger as historian at St Albans monastery in 1235. The historian, W.L. Warren, shows that Roger is not always reliable:

SOURCE 14

Roger of Wendover writes that in 1209 a royal servant, Geoffrey the archdeacon of Norwich . . . held that it was not safe for men in holy orders to serve the king . . . this reached John who, in a fury, sent Sir William Talbot to arrest him. He was imprisoned in chains . . . and deprived of food, so that . . . he died an agonising death. There is undoubtedly something wrong with this story for Geoffrey the archdeacon of Norwich, so far from dying in 1209, became bishop of Ely in 1225.

W.L. Warren, *King John*, 1961

Magna Carta

Towards the end of June 1215 messengers on horseback could be seen riding out from King John's court at Windsor. Their job was to travel to every county and deliver a roll of parchment about 34 cm long and 51 cm wide with the king's Great Seal fixed to the bottom. This document was called a **charter** and people were pleased to get it because they hoped it would put an end to the civil war that had been going on for nearly a year between John and a large group of rebel barons.

> **i Charter** A written document which records a grant of rights given by one person to another. Medieval kings used charters to give land or special privileges to other people. The kings showed they had agreed to a charter by having their Great Seal fixed to the bottom.

Why did the barons want a charter?

The barons' main complaints were that John had demanded too much money from them in taxes to pay for his expensive war against the French king; that the way he decided how much someone should pay was unfair; that those who couldn't pay were brutally punished; and that there was no way for someone who was wrongly treated to complain and ask for compensation.

When the rebels captured London, John agreed to meet them at Runnymede, a large meadow by the river Thames. After about a week of talks he agreed to give the barons a charter saying what he could and could not do in the future. Because it was about their freedoms, the barons called it a 'charter of liberties'. Today it is called 'Magna Carta' which is Latin for 'Great Charter'.

SOURCE 15

This is one of the copies of Magna Carta that King John sent out from Windsor in 1215.

activity

1 Magna Carta had sixty-three sections. You can read some of them in source 17. Each one (except No. 61) is a clue to things that the king must have been doing and the barons felt were wrong or unfair. Use source 17 to work out what those things were.
2 John thought that one section of Magna Carta in particular would make it impossible for him to rule. Look at source 17. Which one do you think it was and why?

SOURCE 16

What did Magna Carta say?

SOURCE 17

John's seal which was attached to Magna Carta.

28. *No constable or other royal official shall take corn or other moveable goods from any man without immediate payment . . .*
38. *In future no official shall place a man on trial unless he can produce believable witnesses to support his accusation.*
39. *No free man shall be seized or imprisoned, or stripped of his rights or possessions, or outlawed or exiled, or deprived of his standing in any other way, nor will we proceed with force against him, or send others to do so, except by the lawful judgement of his equals or by the law of the land.*
40. *To no one will we sell, to no one deny or delay right or justice.*
61. *The barons shall elect twenty-five of their number to keep, and cause to be observed with all their might, the peace and liberties granted and confirmed to them by this charter. Any man may take an oath to obey the commands of the twenty five barons for the achievement of these ends . . .*

Sections from Magna Carta 1215

John's charter did not last very long. Some of the barons never really expected him to keep his word and they were right. John decided that he had given away too much of his power. Within a few weeks civil war had broken out again. In 1216 he died.

John's son Henry was only nine in 1216, so first William Marshal, Earl of Pembroke, and then the justiciar, Hubert de Burgh, ruled for him. One of the first things William did was to re-issue Magna Carta in the name of the new king, Henry III, though he left out some of the sections which he felt were unreasonable from the king's point of view. Without William Marshal Magna Carta would have died with King John.

Source 18 which was written in 1948 is based partly on Magna Carta:

SOURCE 18

Article 3. *Everyone has the right to life, liberty and security of person.*
Article 7. *All are equal before the law and are entitled without any discrimination to equal protection of the law.*
Article 9. *No one shall be subject to arbitrary arrest, detention or exile.*
Article 10. *Everyone is entitled in full equality to a fair and public hearing by an independent and impartial [fair] tribunal [court] . . .*

Articles from the *United Nations Universal Declaration of Human Rights*, 1948

activity

3 Look at source 18. On which sections of Magna Carta (source 17) are these articles based?

assignments

1 Work in pairs to answer these questions:
a Who wanted King John to grant Magna Carta in the first place?
b Which sorts of people benefited from Magna Carta? Which sorts did not?
c Nowadays people often remember Magna Carta as a charter that laid down the rights of ordinary people.
(i) Why is that wrong?
(ii) Why do you think people made that mistake?
Discuss your answers to c with the rest of the class.

2 Why do you think people all over the world think the ideas in Magna Carta are so important?

3 The year 2015 will be the 800th anniversary of Magna Carta. How old will you be then? Imagine that in 2015 a newspaper or magazine asks you to write an article for young people to explain what Magna Carta is and why it is still thought to be so important. Use the information here and any thing else you can find out to write that article.

Parliament

What is Parliament?

Parliament makes the laws that we all have to obey. It consists of the monarch (that is the king or queen), the House of Lords (lords and bishops) and the House of Commons (Members of Parliament – MPs – who are elected by the people).

Today if the **government** wants to make a new law, the Prime Minister has to:

1 Have it written out and take it to the House of Commons. At this stage it is called a 'bill'.
2 Ask the House of Commons to discuss the bill and vote to agree that it should become a law. It must do this three times so that changes can be made.
3 Ask the House of Lords to do the same, also three times.
4 Ask the monarch to sign the bill. When this is done the bill becomes law and is called a 'statute'.

In the Middle Ages, when Parliament began, things were very different. The monarch was the government. There was no Prime Minister; there were no political parties. Today, the monarch

i The **government** is the person or group of people who have the task of ruling a country. Today our government is chosen at a general election. After the election the monarch asks the leader of the political party which has the most MPs to become Prime Minister (head of the government). The Prime Minister then chooses other members of his or her party to become ministers in charge of government departments.

attends Parliament only to declare each session open. In the Middle Ages, Parliament met only when the monarch summoned it to his presence.

How did Parliament begin

Day by day the medieval king took advice from a small council which consisted of those barons and officials who were close to him and travelled with his court. But we know from the Anglo-Saxon Chronicle that William I also made a point of holding three great feasts each year – at Christmas, Easter and Whitsuntide – for his chief barons, bishops and abbots.

As well as being a big social occasion this was a time when they could all join in a 'Great Council' to hear about the king's plans and tell him what they thought. It was at the Great Council of Christmas 1085 that William decided to order the Domesday survey to be carried out.

William's successors followed his example. In time the members of the Great Council expected to be involved in all the king's most important decisions

People first used the word '**parliament**' in the thirteenth century. They didn't mean a place or a body of people like we do today. They just meant a discussion. In particular they meant the discussions held in the Great Councils.

It was in Henry III's reign, sometime around 1258, that people first started to describe the Great Council as 'parliament'. By now it did more than just give advice – if the king wanted to ask people to give him money, he had to tell parliament first and get its agreement.

When the king needed money he usually told the barons, who were the richest people in the country, to give him a certain amount each. But by Henry III's time the barons were insisiting that he should ask them before he did this.

The money that people have to give the government to help to run the country is called a 'tax'. In 1254 Henry found himself so short of money that he decided to ask the knights from the counties to pay him taxes as well as the barons. So he invited them to parliament for the first time, hoping to get their support for this.

His son, Edward I, who had to pay for expensive wars, went even further. He started to invite well-off townspeople, called 'burgesses', to parliament as well.

In fact, it was not Edward, but a baron called Simon de Montefort, who was the first to think of inviting burgesses . In 1265 de Montefort had led a rebellion against Henry III. He decided to call a Great Council of his supporters and had the idea of asking burgesses from the towns that were on his side. Later that year Prince Edward defeated de Montefort and ended the rebellion. When he became king, he borrowed de Montefort's idea.

> **i** **Parliament**   The word 'parliament', or 'parlement', came from an old French word 'parlemenz', meaning 'discussion', which came in turn from 'parler', meaning 'to speak'.

SOURCE 19

A modern photograph of the House of Commons at work.

The king usually asked the knights and burgesses, the 'Commons', to meet separately from the barons and bishops. Edward I did not invite them to all his parliaments but by the time of Edward III (1327–77) they attended nearly every time, and by the end of the fourteenth century they had their own regular meeting place.

SOURCE 20

Edward I in parliament. Find:
- the king
- his two chief vassals, Alexander King of Scots and Llywelyn Prince of Wales. Which is which?
- the Archbishops of Canterbury and York. Which is which?
- the judges (wearing wigs)
- the bishops (wearing tall hats called mitres and black robes)
- the barons (wearing red robes with white fur collars)
- the clerks who wrote down what was said

Who are not shown? Why not?

assignments

1 Parliament in 1377 was different from parliament in 1085.
a How had it changed?
b Was the change rapid or gradual?

2 Make a timeline to run from 1100 to 1300. Put on it all the events that you have read about in Part Two. Use it to help you give a talk, make a diagram or write an article to explain what changed in the way kings governed between 1100 and 1300, and what stayed the same.

3 Find out more about how Parliament works today. What are the differences between now and the time of Edward I? Is anything the same?

Piers Ploughman

In medieval times most people lived and worked in the countryside. When writers and poets wanted to write about a typical Englishman they chose a ploughman. And they gave him a name – **Piers** or Pierce.

Sometime around 1390 a writer finished a new poem. It was written in English, not Latin or French, and people read hand-written copies because printing had not yet been invented. Here is part of the poem:

SOURCE 1

As I went by the way, weeping for sorrow, I saw a poor man hanging on to the plough. His coat was of a coarse stuff [material]; his hood was full of holes and his hair stuck out of it. As he trod the soil his toes stuck out of his worn shoes with their thick soles; his hose [stockings] hung about his hocks [shins] on all sides and he was all bedaubed [covered] with mud as he followed the plough. He had two mittens, scantily made of rough stuff, with worn out fingers and thick with muck.

This man bemired himself in [was covered with] mud almost to the ankle, and drove four heifers [young cows] before him that had become feeble, so that men might count their every rib so sorry-looking they were. His wife walked beside him with a long goad [whip] . . . She went barefoot on the ice so that the blood flowed . . .

Pierce the Ploughman's Creed, c.1390

> **i** **Piers** *was an early form of the French name Pierre which is also the French word for 'rock'. It was a very popular name and people spelt it in lots of different ways, eg. Pierce, Pearce, Petur.*

SOURCE 2

Ploughing. A monk painted this picture in about 1340 in a book called the *Luttrell Psalter*.

In 1005 Aelfric, the Abbot of Eynsham in Oxfordshire, wrote a book of conversations between a teacher and his pupil on one side and people from different jobs on the other. Here the master is talking to a ploughman:

SOURCE 3

Master: *What do you say, ploughman, how do you do your work?*
Ploughman: *Oh, sir, I work very hard. I go out at dawn and I drive the oxen to the field and yoke them to the plough . . . and every day I have to plough a whole **acre** or more. I have a boy who drives the oxen with a goad, and even now he is hoarse with cold and shouting.*

Aelfric, *Colloquy*, 1005

i An **acre** was a rectangular area of land. It was about 200 metres long and about 5 metres wide. It may have been the amount of land that a team could plough in one day. Nowadays an acre refers to the same area of land, but it can be in any shape.

activity

1a How many years separate source 3 from sources 1 and 2?
b What is there in sources 1, 2 and 3 to suggest that very little changed over that time?
2a Look at source 4. How many years separate sources 2 and 4?
b How much appears to have changed over that time?
c How many years separate source 4 and today?
d You would not see the scene in source 4 today. What would you see instead?
3 Which has been the period of greatest change since 1005 according to these sources?

SOURCE 4

Oxen ploughing on the Sussex Downs in about 1900.

Village and manor

Whose plough do you think Piers is using in sources 1 and 2 and whose oxen? Whose land was he ploughing? You may think that they are obviously his plough, his oxen and his land; and you could be right. But it is a lot more likely that he had borrowed the plough and owned only one or two of the oxen. As for whose land he was ploughing, that could depend on what day of the week it was.

Piers lived in a completely different world from ours. The main people in it were his family and neighbours who lived with him in this village, and the lord of the **manor** who expected the villagers to serve him in various ways in return for a house and some land.

The villagers

The villagers could not read or write so they have left no writings of their own to tell us how their world worked or what it was like to live in it. But lords of the manor liked to write down the duties and payments that the people in their manors owed them. These records were written for the lord's use and from his point of view. Even so you can work out a lot about village life from them.

SOURCE 5

Harrowing. This was the next job after ploughing. The harrow broke up the lumps of earth ready for sowing with corn. The man behind the harrow is slinging stones at the crows which are trying to eat the seed. From the *Luttrell Psalter*.

> **i** *A* **manor** was an estate which the owner, who was called the lord or lady of the manor, held in return for giving loyalty and services to an even greater landowner such as a baron. The boundaries of the village and the manor were not always the same. One manor could include more than one village and some villages were split between two manors.

> **i** The **Luttrell Psalter** was a book of psalms specially made for Geoffrey Luttrell who was lord of the manor of Irnham in Lincolnshire. This sort of decoration is known as 'illumination' and books like this are called 'illuminated manuscripts'. You can see the Luttrell Psalter today in the British Library in London.

Sources 6 and 7 come from a record of the work and payments that the villagers of Pytchley in Northamptonshire had to give the lord of the manor in 1125. It comes from a survey of the lands of Peterborough Abbey called *The Black Book of Peterborough*.

SOURCE 6

*There are 9 full **villeins** and 9 **half villeins** and 5 **cottagers**. The full villeins work 3 days a week up to the feast of St Peter in August and thence up to Michaelmas every day by custom, and the half villeins in accordance with their **tenures**; and the cottagers one day a week and two in August. All together they have 8 plough teams.*

The Black Book of Peterborough, 1125

SOURCE 7

Each full villein ought to plough and harrow [see source 5] one acre at the winter ploughing and one at the spring, and winnow [see source 10] the seed in his lord's grange [barn] and sow it. The half villeins do as much as belongs to them. Beyond this they should lend their plough teams three times at the winter ploughing and three times at the spring ploughing and once for harrowing. And what they plough they reap and cart. And they render [give] 5 shillings at Christmas and 32 pence at St Peter's Feast.

*And Agemund the miller renders 26 shillings for his mill and for one **yardland**. And all the villeins render 32 hens at Christmas. The full villeins render 20 eggs and the half villeins 10 eggs and the cottagers 5 eggs at Easter . . . the priest [gives] for the church and 2 yardlands, 5 shillings. Walter the freeman pays 2 shillings for a half yardland. Leofric the smith pays 12 pence [1 shilling] for one **toft**. And Ralf the **sokeman** lends his plough three times a year.*

The Black Book of Peterborough, 1125

SOURCE 8

Reaping with sickles and binding the wheat sheaves. From the *Luttrell Psalter*.

---

i Villein   A villager who farmed about 30 acres of land in return for working for his lord. He was not free.
Half villein   A villein who held a smaller amount of land.
Cottager   A villager, also not free, who had a small house or cottage and a very small amount of land, about 1 to 5 acres. He had to do less work for his lord than a villein because he had less land.
Tenure   The terms on which each tenant held his land.

i Yardland   About 30 acres of land. It was the average amount of land held by a villein. The exact measurement varied from village to village.
Toft   A house with a workshop and a bit of garden.
Sokeman   A freeman who paid the lord a rent for his land and gave occasional services, but who did not have to work for the lord every week like a villein.

activity

1a Did each tenant have his own plough team?
b How do you think a family managed to plough its land if it did not own a full plough team?
2 How much time did full villeins get to work on their own land?
3a Michaelmas was 29 September. Why do you think that all the tenants had to work more days for their lord in August and September? (Source 8 will help you.)
b Why was that particularly inconvenient for them?

SOURCE 9

A woman blacksmith at work. Some historians have said that only men did the job of blacksmiths in the Middle Ages. Why do you think they have said this? Does this picture prove them wrong? What information would you need to be sure?

SOURCE 10

Threshing the sheaves with flails to separate the grain. After that they winnowed the grain by tossing it in a sheet so that the lighter husks, or chaff, blew away in the wind leaving the corn ready to be ground into flour or used as seed for next year's crop. From the *Luttrell Psalter*.

SOURCE 11

This picture from the *Luttrell Psalter* shows villagers taking the corn to the miller to be ground into flour. Unfree peasants had to have their corn ground at the lord's mill. The lord took some of the flour as payment and the miller often cheated them. It was easy to grind corn at home but this was not allowed. Even so people tried to get away with it. The abbot of St Albans paved his private parlour with the millstones he had confiscated from his tenants.

activity

Read source 7 and work in pairs to answer the following questions:

4 The villeins and cottagers had to make three different sorts of payments to the lord in the course of the year. What were they?

5 The men mentioned by name were probably all freemen.

a How did they pay for their land?

b How was that different from the villeins and cottagers?

6 Which villagers did other jobs as well as farming?

7 The smith owned very little land. How do you think he fed and clothed himself and his family?

8 Who paid the highest rent? Why do you think it was so high? (Source 11 will help you.)

Fines and tithes

The lives of ordinary people were controlled by all sorts of rules unless they were lucky enough to be free. Villeins could not leave the village for any reason without the lord's permission and a lord could literally sell a man and his family.

On top of this Piers and all the other unfree men and women in the village had to give their lord all sorts of special payments, or 'fines'. Unfree people had to pay a fine if:

- they sent their son to school
- their daughter got married
- they inherited some land

If an unfree man died his widow had to give:

- her best animal to the lord
- her second best animal to the church
- a fine to the lord when she took over her husband's holding of land

Lords of the manor had records of the fines paid to them written on long pieces of parchment. These were kept rolled up and are known as 'account rolls'.

The village community

Source 13 shows Laxton in Nottinghamshire. It is one of the few places in England that still looks as it did in the Middle Ages. You can see the village houses grouped in the middle

SOURCE 12

A tithe barn. Everyone, free and unfree, had to give 10% of their produce to the church each year. This was called a tithe. In some places the church built tithe barns like this one in Maidstone to store it all.

SOURCE 13

The village and fields of Laxton in Nottinghamshire.

and around them the big open fields ploughed in ridges. You can also see that often several ridges have been grouped together. These groups of ridges are called 'strips'. This is how ordinary people divided up the land.

Instead of owning one or two fields with hedges round them, each person owned strips scattered among three big fields. Even the lord's land was split up like this. The idea was that everyone should have a fair share of the different types of land in the village: good, bad and average. The system also meant that everyone had to plough, sow, harrow and harvest at the same time.

Everyone had to keep the rules. For example, when they had sown one of the big fields, the villagers had to put up a hedge made of dead branches at each end of their strips. All these hedges made one big fence round the field to keep the animals off the crops. If anyone was lazy or careless they could find themselves having to answer to their neighbours in the manor court (source 15).

The villagers appointed one of their number to be 'reeve'. The reeve's job was to organise all the work in the village and to see that everyone carried out their duties for the lord.

You would have found villages that looked like Laxton all over the Midlands and over most of the south of England in the Middle Ages; but not in the north and west. There the villages were smaller and the people fenced in one field, called the 'infield'.

SOURCE 14

Working in the village.

SOURCE 15

Because they did not close their hedges at the proper time, so that the lord and their neighbours received damage, they are enjoined [ordered] under pain of a fine that the hedges be reasonably made within one week.

From the court rolls of Halesowen in Worcestershire, 1281

activity

1 Use the sources in Part 3 so far to make a list of all the various kinds of work done in the village by women. Were there any differences between their work and that of men?

2a What evidence is there from sources 13 and 14 that everybody in the village had to do the same jobs at the same time?

b Why was that so important?

Farming and food

The villagers needed food, shelter, clothes and tools. They had to provide all these themselves from the different sorts of land that they farmed: woods, meadow and fields. On these they could keep animals and grow crops. This sounds simple but people had to live ·with all sorts of problems.

Animals

The kinds of animals that were found on a manor were oxen, cows, sheep and pigs. There were plenty of these on the home farm and each peasant family had some of its own – how many depended on their wealth. Hens were common too. (How can we tell? Look at source 7 on page 40.)

The first problem was how to feed cattle in the winter. Oxen and cows like to eat hay, which is dried meadow grass, in the winter. People did not know that you could sow grass as a crop, so the only hay they had was what was mowed in June in the natural meadows that grew in most villages near the stream. These meadows were not large and had to supply the whole village. Each family had very little hay which meant they could not have many cattle. They could give their cattle oats, barley or beans, but then they might not have enough for the family.

The last choice was to kill the animals around Christmas . That way a family would also have some meat to eat. The problem with this was that the oxen were needed to pull the plough and the cows for milk. They couldn't really afford to kill them. When they did kill animals, such as pigs, they had no good way of preserving the meat so they had to eat it soon afterwards anyway.

Crops

The villagers knew about two kinds of crops – the ones like wheat which they sowed in the autumn and harvested in August, and the ones like oats, peas, beans and barley which they sowed in the spring and also harvested in August or September. But there was a problem here too: the more they used a piece of ground, the more the soil became exhausted and it produced a smaller crop each time around. They knew that dung from animals would fertilise the ground; but the villagers had too few animals to produce enough dung to do the job properly. The other way they knew to restore the soil was to leave it unused for a year. This was called 'lying fallow'.

activity

1 Look at source 17. The boxes at the bottom show the main things the villagers needed. The others show what they had on their farms. Some of the boxes have been joined up by a line with a label to show how they link. Copy the diagram and then add as many more links and labels as you can.
2 Use sources 16, 17 and the information in the text to say why **a** meadows, and **b** woods were very important to the villagers.

SOURCE 16

Beating down acorns to fatten the pigs. What are the differences between these pigs and the ones on farms today?

SOURCE 17

The village's needs and resources.

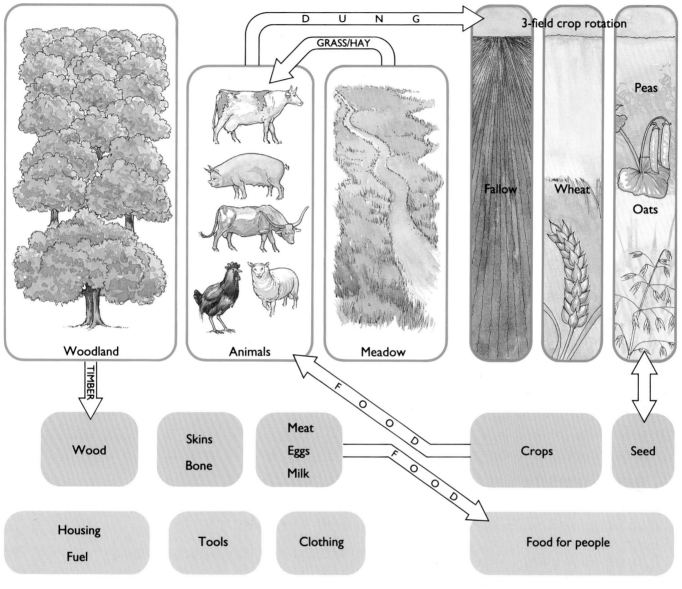

KEY

☐ resources

▢ products

▢ uses/things people needed

In many places the villagers would have used a system called a 'three-year rotation' to be able to grow the most crops possible on their land. They grouped all the ploughed land in the village into three very large fields. Then they used each field in a different way each year. They sowed the first one with wheat in the autumn; the second with oats, peas and so on in the spring; and the third they left fallow all year. They swapped the way they used the fields so that each lay fallow once every three years. Source 17 shows how the system worked. They grazed their animals on the fallow field so as to fertilise it with dung.

In the smaller villages of the north and west of England, the villagers used their one field, the infield (see page 42), for several years without letting it lie fallow. Then they abandoned it and fenced in a new one.

ℹ **Piers the Ploughman** was written by William Langland sometime between 1370 and 1390. Piers is the hero of the poem which shows all sorts of people searching for the way to live a good life.

Feeding the family

It could be difficult getting enough food for the family, especially at certain times of the year:

SOURCE 18

I have no penny quoth [says] Piers pullets [small hens] for to buy
Nor neither geese nor piglets but two fresh cheeses
A few curds and cream and an oaten cake
And two loaves of beans and bran to bake for my little ones
And besides I say by my soul I have no salt bacon
Nor no little eggs, by Christ, collops [meals] for to make
But I have parsley and leeks and many cabbages
And by this livelihood we must live till Lammas [1 August] time.

William Langland, *Piers the Ploughman*, c.1380

activity

1 Read source 18. Piers is speaking in the spring.
Why is Lammas so important? What will he have to eat then?
2 Use what you have found out about farming and food in medieval times to make a list of all the reasons why you think Piers and his family never had enough to eat in the spring.

assignments

1 Use sources 1, 6, 7, 10, 11, 13, 14 and 15 to describe:
a the ways in which village life in the Middle Ages was very hard.
b how people worked together and supported one another.

2a Look at source 14. How does it help us to understand how the village community worked?
b Give one example from Part 3 of the following kinds of source: a manor survey; a poem; a court roll; an illuminated manuscript.
c Which do you think is the most useful in helping us to find out about the life of villagers in the Middle Ages?
d Which is the least useful?

3 The villagers of the Middle Ages did not eat what we call a 'balanced diet'. Find out what a 'balanced diet' means and what food experts recommend it should be. Use the information in Part 3 to work out how the villagers' diet fell short of this and how this affected them. Write up your findings in the form of a report.

Markets

activity

3 Here is a list of some things which families need:

food	saucepans
clothes	plates
drink	knives
furniture	towels
curtains	soap

a Make three columns, one headed 'Make or grow', one headed 'Buy or rent' and one headed 'Swap'.
b Now put each of the items from the list to the column that is correct for your family. Some things may need to go in more than one column, for example, you might grow some food in your garden.
c Think of two more items of your own to go into each column and write them in.
d Which column has most in it? Is that what you would expect? Why?
e See if other people have come up with the same results.

If you need something that you haven't got, you have three choices:

- you can make it or grow it for yourself
- you can buy it or rent it
- you can swap something you don't need in exchange for the thing that you do need

There is a fourth choice which is that you can persuade someone to give it to you as a present; but you have to be lucky to do that very often, so we'll leave that one out.

Some people are self-sufficient. That means they make and grow everything they need for themselves. There are some parts of the world today where people are self-sufficient; but not nearly as many as in medieval times when most villagers had to live that way. But it is very rare for people to be completely self-sufficient. Even Piers Ploughman and his family needed things that they could not provide for themselves – in particular, salt to help them preserve meat in winter and iron for plough-shares and other tools. Piers probably thought of salt and iron as essentials. Essentials are things you cannot do without. They are necessary for your survival. There may be other things you would like, but they are luxuries. Luxuries are things that you do not need in order to survive, but which make life a lot more enjoyable.

activity

4 Make two columns, one headed 'Essential', the other headed 'Luxury'.
a Decide which column each of the following should go into and write them in:

jewellery	drink	paper	cooker	clothing
house or flat	books	chair	knife	plate
television	food	piano	shoes	saucepan
central heating	matches			

b See if other people agree with your decisions.
5a Would you be happy to lead a life in which you could have only the essentials and none of the luxuries?
b Do you think ordinary people in the Middle Ages were happy with that way of life? Explain your reasons.
6 What do you think makes it possible for people to have luxuries?

i **Peasant** means someone who lives in the country and works on the land. The English first used the word in the fifteenth century. It came from the Old French word 'paisant' which in turn came from the Latin word 'pagus' meaning country district.

Money or exchange

It was the same for people in the Middle Ages as it is for us now: if you needed something that you could not make or grow for yourself you had to get it from someone else. For this to be possible you had to have either some money to spend or something to exchange.

You have already found out that most **peasants** did not earn money. They paid for things like their land and their taxes either by giving their labour or by giving some of their goods. By the time they had done this they had very little, if anything, left over. Something that is left over is called a 'surplus'. If a peasant had a surplus it meant that he or she had something to exchange or to sell. Cottagers and half villeins did not often have a surplus, but some of the better-off villeins may sometimes have had one, and the lord of the manor certainly did.

So there were always some people in the countryside with goods to exchange or sell, and who were looking for the essentials and luxuries that would make their lives better. They needed a place, not too far from their village, where they could meet other people with the same idea. That place was called a market. One market served several villages and people usually met there once a week on 'market day'.

Market day

A medieval market was very like a street market today. People set up stalls, sometimes with awnings, or else they spread out what they had to sell on a box or table, or on the ground.

SOURCE 19

The fish stall.

SOURCE 20

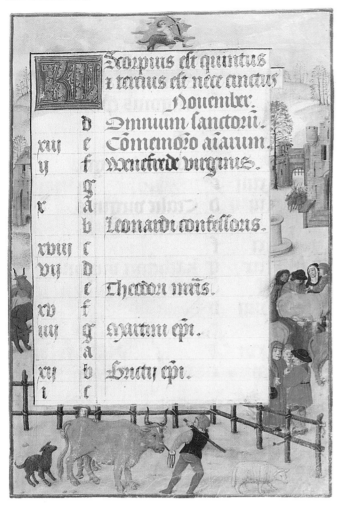

Taking a cow to market.

SOURCE 22

A pedlar. Some pedlars travelled around the villages as well as selling at markets and fairs.

SOURCE 21

Buying and selling clothes. What do you think is happening in this picture?

activity

la Suppose you are the peasant with the cow in source 20 and that you want to exchange it for some iron so that you can make some tools. When you meet the person selling iron you find that he or she doesn't want a cow.
What do you do?

b How is it easier to use money to pay for goods instead of having to buy and sell by exchanging goods and arguing about their values?

Markets usually grew up at cross-roads or beside rivers at places which boats could reach. Why do you think this was? The number of markets grew steadily as people found they needed or could afford more things. Storeholders like a shoemaker usually made the things they sold themselves. As people wanted to buy more things, more craftspeople were needed to make them.

It made sense for the men and women who made things to sell in the market to set up their workshops close to where the market was held. They worked in little rooms that opened on to the street and gradually the owners turned their workshops into shops, with counters at the front and a place to make things at the back.

SOURCE 23

A covered market in the fifteenth century.

SOURCE 24

A street with shops. Find:
- the tailor
- the barber
- the seller of furs
- the pharmacist, who prepares and sells medicines and drugs

activity

1 What are the differences between the fifteenth-century market scene shown in source 23 and the scenes from at least a hundred years before shown in sources 21 and 22?

2 What are the differences between sources 23 and 24?

The town

Most places where markets were held ended up turning into towns. The craftspeople who made things to sell in the market needed to live and work around it. They also needed the market to buy the food that they hadn't the time or the space to grow for themselves. Source 25 shows what a typical English town looked like in about 1340. Find:

- the walls and towers
- the gates. How many are there?
- the large church
- the windmill (beside the church)
- the houses. What materials are they made of?
- the poles sticking up from the houses. The signs hanging from them advertised the trade of the people living there. For instance a tavern always showed a broom. How many taverns can you see?
- the band, the dancers and the people watching

The merchants and craftspeople who lived and worked in towns needed to be freemen, not serfs or villeins. They needed to be able to buy and sell land in the town, to make agreements or contracts with one another and to make rules for the running of the town.

activity

3 What evidence is there that people living in towns wanted to be free to get on with their business in safety and security?

4a Make a list of all the things that you think a town needed from the surrounding countryside.

b What effect do you think that had on the people who lived in the countryside? Which ones benefited?

5 What jobs, apart from making and selling goods for the market, do you think a town had to offer?

SOURCE 25

A painting of a town from the *Luttrell Psalter*. The artist painted this to show his idea of the city of Constantinople (in modern Turkey) but he had never been there so he used an English town as a model.

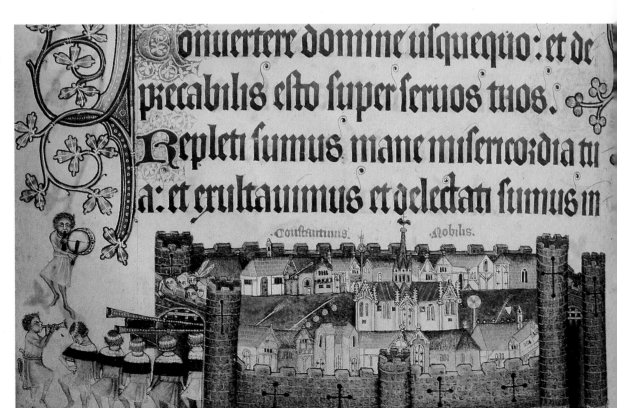

All this meant that it was no good if they had to obey a lord of the manor. So the people of the town usually asked the king to grant the town a charter in return for a payment of money. The charter said that they were free to do all these things. It also allowed them to pay their taxes to the king in one fixed lump sum each year and to decide for themselves how much each citizen should contribute towards this. Usually the freemen, or burgesses, elected a council from among themselves to run the town's affairs.

Living and working in towns

The English first started to use surnames sometime after 1200. The names tell us the craft or trade of their owners. Here are the names of some of the people living in Colchester in the early fourteenth century:

Tanner	Tyler	Miller	Smith
Taylor	Weaver	Fisher	Butcher
Carpenter	Baker	Spicer	Fuller
Mason	Mariner	Wright	Cook

What was the craft or trade of each of the owners of these names? Look up the ones you don't know in a dictionary.

Young people who wanted to learn a craft or trade had to ask someone already experienced in it to teach them. In return for a sum of money, they joined their teacher's family as an apprentice for a set number of years. After that they joined a craft 'gild'. By the middle of the fourteenth century a man could not work at his craft unless he belonged to the gild. Women worked at all sorts of crafts and trades but do not appear to have belonged to gilds:

SOURCE 27

If any married woman follow a craft within the city, which her husband has nothing to do with, she shall be counted as a sole [unmarried] woman in connection with anything to do with her craft. And if a complaint is made against her, she shall answer it as a sole woman.

From the town laws of Lincoln

SOURCE 26

The first letter of Edward III's charter to the town of Bristol, given in 1347. Find the pictures inside the letter 'a'. They tell you about some of the things that town councils had to see to. The top one shows wrong-doers being locked up and the bottom one shows a baker being dragged through the streets sitting on a hurdle. The scales above him show that he has been caught selling bread that was under weight for the price he charged.

activity

1 The Lincoln rule about married women (source 27) was probably made to protect a husband from having to pay up if his wife made a mistake or owed money in her business.
a What does it tell you about the usual relationship of husband and wife in medieval times?
b Why was this rule good for the husband?
c Do you think it was good or bad for the wife?

There was always work for builders in towns – both carpenters and stonemasons. Medieval pictures of stonemasons at work usually show only men. But we know that women must have done the work too because at least one, a German called Sabina von Steinbach, reached the highest rank of master mason. Around 1300 she was given the contract to be master mason at Strasbourg Cathedral which meant she had to design the building and supervise all the work.

SOURCE 28

Stonemasons, about 1250. Find:
- the scaffolding
- the ladder
- the pulley

What jobs are the masons doing and what tools are they using? What would be much the same on a building site today? What would be different?

SOURCE 29

Carpenters making a wooden frame for a house, about 1430. Find:
- a box of iron nails. What are they being used for?
- wooden pegs. What are they being used for?
- a plane
- a saw
- drills, axes and hammers

What other tools can you see? Are there any differences between these tools and the ones carpenters use today?

SOURCE 30

The wage per day for various kinds of worker in about 1300:

Worker	Daily rate
Skilled worker *(eg carpenter or mason)*	3–4d.(pence)
Unskilled labourer	1–1½d.
Reaper and helper *(reaping and binding an acre of wheat, a day's work for two people)*	5d.
Thatcher and helper	3d.

SOURCE 31

The cost of food in 1300:

Item	Cost
30–40 eggs	1d.
3–4 pigeons	1d.
1 lb cheese	1d.
1 hen	1¼d.
1 fat pig	36d.

activity

1 Use sources 30 and 31 to answer these questions:
a Which workers were best paid?
b Which were worst paid?
c Is it true that town workers were always paid better that country workers?
d Do you think these workers were paid enough to live off?
2 In 1900 a farm worker was paid 2 shillings (24d.) a day and that would buy 40 eggs then, so a farmworker in 1900 earned more than a farmworker in 1300. Did the change in wages mean that life had got any better?

Sports and pastimes

SOURCE 32

Every year on the day called 'Carnival' scholars from the different schools bring fighting cocks to their masters, and the whole morning is set apart to watch the cocks do battle, for the boys are given a holiday that day. After dinner all the young men of the town go out into the fields in the suburbs to play ball.

On feast days throughout the summer the young men play the sports of archery, jumping, wrestling, slinging the stone, hurling the javelin and fighting with sword and buckler [small round shield].

In winter on almost every feast day before dinner, either foaming boars fight for their lives 'to save their bacon' or stout bulls or huge bears do battle with the hounds let loose upon them. When the great marsh that washes the north wall of the city is frozen over, swarms of young men go to play games on the ice.

William fitz Stephen, *Description of London*, 1171

activity

3 Look at sources 32 to 34.
a Which of these sports and pastimes still go on today?
b Which of them are not allowed today? What does that tell you about the differences between the Middle Ages and today?

SOURCE 33

Punch and Judy.

SOURCE 34

Cock Fighting.

assignments

1 Towns changed the way people lived. This is called 'social' change. They also changed the way they earned their money. This is called 'economic' change. Here is an example of each:

Social change	**Economic change**
Joined gilds	Made things to sell

Find as many more examples of each kind of change as you can.

2 Design and make a large chart or display, with pictures, to show all the ways in which the people of a medieval town used the countryside around it and the people of the countryside used the town.

3 Suppose you are a labourer in medieval times. Would you rather live in a village or in a town? Explain each of your reasons carefully.

4 Where is your local market? Find out how long it has been there. Where do the things the traders sell come from? What is similar to a medieval market? What is different?

4
Making and Trading

Making

If you take some pieces of wood and make them into a table, the table that you finish up with is of more use and value to you than the pieces of wood with which you started. You have used your skill and time to turn something that is of less use and value (the wood) into something that is of more use and value (the table). The wood is what's called the 'raw material' and the table is the 'finished product'.

A lot of men and women in the Middle Ages used their skill and time to make the things that they needed for themselves or that other people wanted. Here are some examples:

SOURCE 1

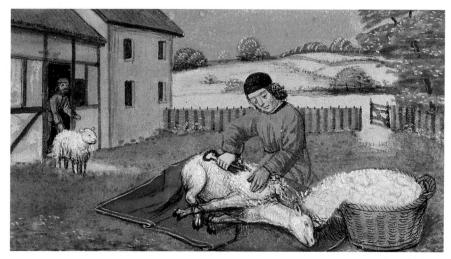

England was the main wool producing country in the Middle Ages. This farmer is shearing the wool fleece off a sheep. Find:
- the shears. How do they work?
- the binding round the sheep's legs. What is it for?
- the sheet to prevent any wool being lost. What does that tell you about wool?

SOURCE 2

The women are making linen from the fibres of a plant called 'flax'. Find:
- the woman on the right who is pulling the raw flax into sections
- the woman next to her who is 'carding' the flax by combing it out into strands
- the 'spinster'. Her job is to put the flax onto the end of the spindle and then draw out the fibres into a thread with her left hand
- the weaver. She is weaving the threads into linen cloth on the handloom at the back

activity

Look at sources 1–6.
1 Which ones show people working to provide raw materials?
2 Which ones show people using raw materials to make things?

SOURCE 3

The process of dyeing cloth. In the Middle Ages people liked strong bright colours. Blue, black, red and yellow dyes could be made from plants that grew in England; but some colours had to be imported from abroad. Find:
- the big tub, or 'vat', containing the dye
- the fire to heat the vat
- the wood for the fire
- the cloth waiting to be dyed
- the finished cloth

SOURCE 5

Part of a brass monument made in 1463. It shows an iron-miner in the Forest of Dean in England. This area had been producing iron since Roman times, but a lot more had to be imported from countries across the Channel. Find:
- the miner's pick
- his candle
- his 'hod' – the basket on his back for carrying the iron ore he has dug out

SOURCE 4

A glass-blowing works in Bohemia. Find:
- the workers digging and carrying sand, the raw material for making glass
- the furnace for making the glass
- the glass-blower
- the worker checking the finished items
- the worker packing them to be carried off for sale

SOURCE 6

The artist is painting a religious picture. These were very popular in the Middle Ages and were sold all over Europe. Find:
- the box of brushes and the paints. What are they kept in?
- the apprentice. What is he doing?
What does the fact that she has an apprentice tell you about the artist?

Trading

You found out in Part 3 that the people who made things in the Middle Ages were very often also the people who sold them. They lived and worked near markets and often towns grew up around them.

But there was always room for men and women who made a living not out of making and selling, but simply out of buying and selling. These people were traders, or merchants, and as time passed they became more numerous and more prosperous. By the fifteenth century some English merchants were wealthier than some barons.

SOURCE 7

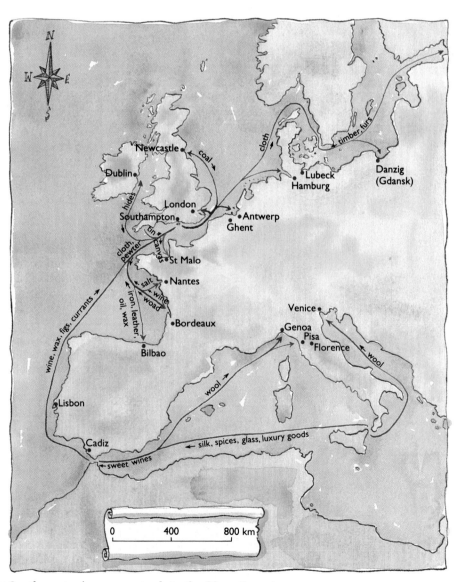

Southampton's overseas trade in the fifteenth century.

The process of making involves turning raw materials of less use and value into finished products of more use and value. The process of trading involves moving things from places where they are of less value to where they are of more value. This could mean taking a raw material such as wool from the farmer who has produced the wool to the cloth-maker who is going to turn it into cloth; or it could involve taking a finished product such as the cloth to someone who wants to buy it.

Merchants specialise in buying something cheaply in one place and selling it for a profit in another.

The merchants of Southampton

The merchants of Southampton, like those of all the big English ports, traded all over Europe as well as in England itself.

Two well known Southampton merchants in the thirteenth century were the 'Femmes Soles' Petronilla la Fleming and Dame Claramunda who, in 1258, won the contract to supply the king with wine from France.

A typical Southampton merchant of the fifteenth century was Walter Fetplace who bought woad, a dye, and alum, which was used for making cloth, from the Italians and sent it to towns such as Salisbury and Winchester where cloth was made. There he bought wool and cloth to sell back to the Italians. Like most merchants he dealt in all sorts of goods (such as wine, fish, fruit and salt) as well as specialising in things to do with cloth-making.

The merchant business

SOURCE 8

Remember envy is more general in all men's hearts than is commonly believed and so you will not err [make a mistake] in ever keeping your business secret and not making a show of it, and not speaking in your shop of your profits or your riches. To confide in a man is to turn yourself into his slave.

From a book by an Italian merchant called Paolo da Certaldo

i **Femmes Soles** *were legally independent women, married or single, who had the right to trade on their own account.*

activity

2 Work in groups of three or four. Your task is to plan how you would set up a business to buy things cheaply and sell them at a profit. You must make realistic decisions about how your group would really go about doing this. You must answer these questions:

a What will you buy and sell?

b Who will you buy it from and who will you sell it to?

c Where will you get the money from to buy the goods in the first place?

d What evidence do you have that any one wants what you have to sell?

e What will it cost (i) to buy the goods in the first place, and (ii) to transport them to where you will sell them?

f How much of your time will all this take up?

g What other costs might you have?

h What price will you sell at? Is it a fair price?

i What profit will you make?

j Will it be worth it?

activity

1 Look at source 8. Do you agree with Paolo da Certaldo? Explain your reasons.

SOURCE 9

Pack horses.

SOURCE 11

Robbing a traveller.

SOURCE 10

Loading a ship with wool.

Anyone setting out to be a merchant in the Middle Ages had to make the same decisions as you did in question 2 on page 59. It was a risky business. It always involved journeys – often very long ones. A lot could go wrong.

There were two main ways of carrying loads – packhorse (source 9) and ship (source 10). Packhorses could be ambushed (source 11) and ships might run into storms or be attacked by pirates. So a merchant could lose something every time goods were sent out. By the end of the fourteenth century most merchants took out insurance:

SOURCE 12

Touching [about] your saying the ship has reached Barcelona safely, you are no prophet – and if some evil had come to her, it would have been the worse for you. For you have our orders never to send any merchandise of ours without insurance, and let this be said to you once and for all.

A letter from Francesco Datini to his partner in Genoa, 1398

activity

1 Look at source 12.
a What has Datini's partner done wrong?
b How important does Datini think this is? How can you tell?
2 Look at source 13. Do you think the instructions of the merchant in Avignon to his assistant are fair on the artist who paints the picture? Explain your reasons.

Journeys were generally slow and expensive. A merchant could not afford to allow a packhorse or a ship to travel out fully laden in one direction and come back empty in the other. So they were always on the lookout for chances to buy new goods cheaply where they had just sold something at a profit:

SOURCE 13

You tell me you can find no pictures for the money we will pay, for there are none that cheap. Therefore we bid you, if you find no good things at fair cost, leave them, for here there is no great demand. They should be bought when the artist who makes them is in need.

A letter from a merchant in Avignon to his assistant in Florence, 1387

Someone starting out as a merchant always has the problem of finding the money to buy goods to trade with in the first place. Money for this purpose is called 'capital'. One way to raise capital is to sell something that you already have, perhaps some land. Another way is to borrow the money and pay interest on the loan until you can pay it back.

However, in the Middle Ages the Church taught that it was a sin to make a profit without doing any work or sharing in the risks of work. So Christians were not allowed to make money out of lending it. Until the thirteenth century the main money lenders were Jews who were not Christians and so did not have to worry about the rules of the Church.

By the fourteenth century many Christian merchants were very rich and were even being asked to lend money to kings. Many of them set up a bank as part of their business to deal with money lending (source 14). By the fifteenth century the Church no longer minded.

The main things that English merchants traded abroad were wool and cloth. Source 15 is about wool:

SOURCE 15

Right-worshipful sir, I humbly recommend myself to you. My master has shipped his fells [fleeces] which you must receive and pay the freight [for the transport]. First by the grace of God, in the 'Mary' of London, William Sordvale master, 7 packs, lying by aft [behind] the mast, one pack lyeth up rest [on top] and some of that pack is summer fells marked with an O. . . . Item, in the 'Thomas' of Maidstone, Harry Lawson master, 6 packs whereof [of which] lyeth 5 packs next before the mast under hatched, and one pack lyeth in the stern sheet [inside the boat at the back]. Item, Sir, ye shall also receive in the 'Mary', Rainham, John Danyell master, your trunk with your glass and an Essex cheese.

A letter to an English merchant in Calais in 1481

SOURCE 14

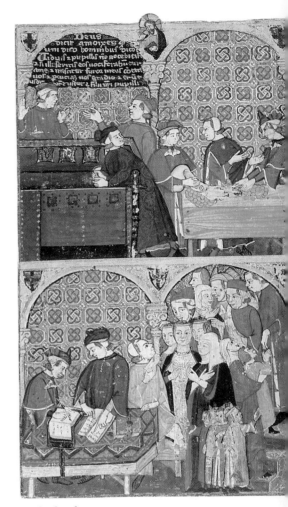

At the bank.

activity

3 Look at source 15.
a How many different ships does the letter mention?
b Which ports are the ships coming from?
c Where are these ports? Use an atlas to help you to find them.
d Why do you think the merchant in England used more than one port?
e What evidence is there that the merchant in Calais lives near Rainham?
f Why do you think the letter explains so carefully where packs have been stowed in each ship?

SOURCE 16

Francesco Datini. A detail from a religious painting.

'In the name of God and profit'

These were the words written on the first page of the account books of Francesco Datini, a merchant from Prato in Italy.

By the time of his death in 1410 Datini had trading companies in Avigon in France; in Prato, Pisa, Florence and Genoa in Italy; in Barcelona in Spain; and on the island of Majorca. Among other things, he traded in armour, swords, daggers and lances; leather saddles and harnesses; silk curtains, table cloths and towels; painted storage boxes and jewel cases; and religious pictures. He was involved with cloth-making and he bought a lot of his wool from England.

Datini ran each company with partners who worked where the company was based while he stayed in Prato or Florence. Each company also employed a manager, cashiers who wrote up the accounts in large books, and shop boys, office boys and messengers. There were also the apprentices, often sons of friends of Datini, who aimed to become at least managers and preferably partners.

SOURCE 17

Think day and night what you have to do . . . and make a note of what you cannot keep in mind . . . It is not possible to remember all that one has to do, but one should always keep one's mind on what is most needful [necessary].

From an undated letter from Datini to a new cashier in Pisa

SOURCE 18

He does nothing but write, day and night, yet cannot do half the great writings that have piled up during his time away. But he shall not get up from his seat until all is done.

From a letter from Datini in 1381, about one of his junior cashiers in Avignon

SOURCE 19

My Checco went to Paradise a few days ago. It was not from lack of care, for two good doctors were at his bedside . . . It is a great grief to me; he was a good young man and faithful.

From a letter from Datini to his wife, Margherita, in 1380, about a shop boy

SOURCE 20

You are my son . . . do your duty well, and you will acquire honour and profits, and can count on me as if I were your father. But if you do not . . . it will be as if I had never known you.

From a letter from Datini to a new apprentice in Barcelona

activity

1 What do sources 17–20 tell you about **a** what Datini expected of his employees and **b** the way he treated them?

activity

2 What picture of Datini in 1391 do you get from source 21?

3 Read source 22. What has changed by 1401?

4 What clues are there in source 22 as to why the change has taken place? Look at source 21 again. What else might have contributed to the change?

Datini spent most days writing letters to his partners and managers and reading the letters they sent to him. He grew rich by hard work and attention to the minutest detail. His wife, Margherita, and his best friend, Ser Lapo Mazzei, a lawyer, endlessly urged him to work less hard and to spend more time thinking about how to lead a good life. When he died, he left all his money to the poor people of Prato.

SOURCE 21

When I think of the house you are building, of your warehouses in far-off lands, your banquets and your accounts . . . they seem to me to be far beyond what is needful.

I wish you would wind up some of your business matters . . . and give away some of your riches . . . I ask you not to become a priest or a monk, but I say to you: put some order in your life.

Letter from Ser Lapo Mazzei to Datini, 1391

SOURCE 22

You take no account of time and remember not that you must die . . . you count your fingers and say, 'In so much time I shall have made so much' . . . But you remember not our five men who died [of the plague] in this same year . . . I do otherwise: I give more thought to how matters will go after my death, than to those of this world.

Letter from Datini to one of his partners, 1401

assignments

1 Use everything you have found out in this unit to make two lists:
a) of the skills a person needed to have in order to succeed in the business of being a merchant in medieval times; and
b) of the personal qualities that you think he or she needed to have. Explain why you have put each item in your lists.

2 Here are four kinds of source that you can find in Part 4: pictures; maps; merchants' letters; other people's letters. How useful is each one in helping you work out the skills a person needed to be a successful merchant? List them 1 to 4 in order of usefulness and write a few sentences about each one to say why you think it deserves that place in the list.

5

The Age of Faith

In the Middle Ages nearly everybody believed in the existence of the Christian God and in the teachings of the Christian Church.

If you believe in the truth of a religious teaching, you have 'faith' in it. Faith means belief. It has another meaning too. If you trust someone completely, if you have confidence in them and know they will never let you down, then you have 'faith' in them. Faith also means trust.

People in the Middle Ages had faith in both ways – they believed in the truth of Christianity and they trusted in it completely. That is why the Middle Ages are often called the 'Age of Faith'.

The area where Christianity was most popular was called

SOURCE 1

A medieval map showing Jerusalem at the centre of the world. A map like this was called a 'Mappa Mundi' which is Latin for 'map of the world'. This one was made in the thirteenth century. You can see it today at Hereford Cathedral.

SOURCE 3

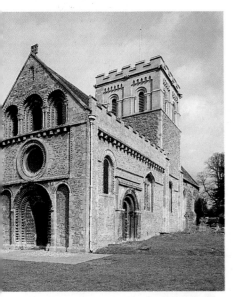

The twelfth-century church at Iffley, Oxford.

Christendom and in the Middle Ages Christendom was mainly based in Europe (see the map on page 8). In other parts of the world at that time people believed in different faiths just as firmly. Islam was the religion of the Arab empire which stretched from the south of Spain to India. In India itself the great religions were Hinduism and Buddhism, which had spread throughout Tibet, China and South East Asia as well. Throughout Europe there were also Jews whose religion was Judaism.

The Christians living in Christendom saw the world entirely from their point of view. They even drew maps (source 1) showing Jerusalem, the city where Christ lived and died, at the centre of the world.

In 1095 Pope Urban II used this idea when he preached a sermon calling Christian kings and knights to go on a **crusade**:

SOURCE 2

This royal city [Jerusalem] ... situated at the centre of the world, is now held captive by God's enemies ...

Fulcher of Chartres, *Historia Hierosolymitana*, 1105

Pope Urban wanted them to recapture Jerusalem and the Holy Land, which had become part of the Arab empire, and return them to Christendom.

The Church and the people

Source 3 shows one of the hundreds of parish churches built in the Middle Ages. The people of Iffley probably helped to build it themselves. Every Sunday they went there to attend **Mass**.

The parish priest who took the service was probably one of the few educated people in the parish and often the only one who could read. He took the service in Latin. The people in the congregation knelt or sat on the floor (not many churches had seats or pews) and listened to the familiar Latin words which they knew off-by-heart but did not understand. The priest did not often preach a sermon – so how did people have any idea of what they were supposed to do or believe as a result of being Christians?

If you go inside one of the 10,000 surviving medieval churches in Britain today it will probably strike you as a cool and quiet place where the chief colour is usually the grey of the ancient stonework. But in medieval times the scene was very different – the walls and pillars would have been covered in bright paint. Much of the

Stained glass *The glass workers started by designing a picture and working out the size and colour of each small piece of glass needed for it. Then they cut the pieces from clear glass, painted them and heated them in a kiln, or furnace, where the chemicals in the paint fused with the glass to colour it. Finally they slotted the pieces of coloured glass into lead strips held together by an iron frame which fitted into the window itself.*

medieval decoration has now disappeared, but some of the wall paintings and many of the **stained-glass** windows have survived. The pictures were messages to the people to tell them how the Church wanted them to behave and what it wanted them to believe.

SOURCE 4

A parish priest pictured in a stained-glass window in All Saints' Church, York.

SOURCE 5

The sin of idle gossip. Priests were always telling people off for talking during sermons.

SOURCE 6

An angel tells the shepherds of the birth of Jesus.

SOURCE 7

Heaven and Hell. Find:
- the people trying to climb the ladder to Heaven. The ones who fail to keep their eyes on God (at the top) are pulled into Hell by demons
- the people being forked into a boiling pot
- the people being tortured by having to work on upturned spikes
- the flames of Hell burning people up
- St Michael weighing people's souls to see if they are good enough to go to Heaven. If not, a demon will take them to Hell
- the angel who is helping people out of the 'mouth' of Hell into Heaven

SOURCE 8

Visiting prisoners. One of the 'acts of mercy' which the Church encouraged people to perform.

activity

1 Make lists of all the things that sources 4–8 were telling people that **a** they should believe, **b** they should do, and **c** they should not do. What rewards and punishments were they offering?

Pilgrimages

A pilgrimage is a journey made to a place believed to be holy. People from all walks of life went on pilgrimages in the Middle Ages. Some went to ask forgiveness for their sins; some went to pray for a special favour; some went simply to show their devotion to God and to give thanks.

The holiest place of all was the Holy Land where Jesus lived and died. After that came Rome, the home of the Pope, and the place where St Peter, St Paul and many other famous **saints** were buried. But not many people could afford the journey to these far away places, so most English pilgrims travelled to holy places in their own country.

Most of these were churches where there was a shrine, which was either a tomb containing the body of a saint or a box that held something that belonged to a saint, such as some hair, a bone, or a piece of clothing. People believed that these shrines had miraculous powers and could cure diseases. The shrines themselves were covered with offerings left as thanksgivings by grateful pilgrims.

i **Saint** Someone officially declared by the Church to have lived such a holy life that Christians should pay them special honour and respect.

SOURCE 9

Many people who suffered from a disease or disability painfully made their way to seek a miracle cure at the shrine of a saint.

SOURCE 10

Places of pilgrimage in England.

Offerings list

Some of the offerings found by the Pope's commissioners at the shrine of Thomas Cantilupe, 29 August 1307:
- 129 silver images of various human limbs
- 436 wax images of men
- 1,200 wax images of human limbs
- 108 walking sticks
- 520 gold or silver rings
- an uncountable number of wax images of ears, eyes and teeth.

Holy Days and Festivals

The Church set aside certain days in the year as special feast days or festivals, called holy days. Our word 'holiday' means holy day. On these days most people had the day off and joined in the celebrations.

Some festivals such as May Day (1 May) with its maypole dancing were traditional celebrations which were far older than Christianity. Others such as the Loaf-Mass, or Lammas (1 August), changed an ancient custom into a Christian feast. The ancient custom had been to bury a loaf of bread in the first furrow ploughed after the harvest. At the festival which replaced it, the priest celebrated Mass with the first loaf made from the newly harvested corn.

activity

1a Make a list of the holidays and festivals that you and your family celebrate.
b What other festivals do you know of that are celebrated by other people?

Christmas

The Church's chief festivals were Easter and Christmas. The word 'Christmas' comes from the old English words 'Christes maesse'. Maesse meant 'feast day', so Christmas meant 'Christ's feast day'.

SOURCE 11

These people are taking part in a Mummers Play at Christmas. These plays began in Britain long before Christianity arrived and took place at the time of the winter solstice. The plays were about a fight between a hero and a villain, the death of the hero and then his cure and return to life.

The Feast of the Nativity

In about 300 the Church decided to have a feast day for Christ's birthday. It was called 'Nativitas' in Latin. From this came the English word 'nativity'. No one knew the real date of Jesus's birthday, so the Church chose 25 December as the feast day. The first written record of the celebration of the Feast of the Nativity is from the year 336.

Mid-winter feasts

There were four feasts already happening in December and January long before the Church added Christmas. Gradually Christmas borrowed some of their customs.

The Winter Solstice: As the days get shorter in winter, the sun sinks lower in the sky until it almost looks as if it is standing still. Then the days get longer as spring approaches. This is called the winter solstice which comes from the Latin 'sun [sol] stands still [stitium]'. From early times it has been an important time for religious ceremonies.

The Saturnalia: This was a Roman feast for the god Saturn who was the god of good crops. His feast took place in late December. During this feast slaves were served meals by their masters; people gave each other thin wax candles, called tapers, and children were given clay dolls. There were banquets and decorations of laurel.

The Kalends: This Roman feast took place on the first day of January. It marked the day when important officials took up their jobs for the new year. Again there were banquets and decorations of laurel and lighted tapers. People gave each other good luck presents of figs, honey, pastry or coins.

Yule: This feast took place in northern countries for twelve days in December during the winter solstice. It marked the end of the old year and the start of the new. There was feasting and decorations of holly, mistletoe and lighted tapers.

Christmas in the Middle Ages

Source 13 describes Christmas at the house of a woman whose husband had died shortly before:

SOURCE 13

There were no disguisings [acting], nor harping, nor singing and no loud sports. Only playing at the tables [board games] and chess and cards which sports she gave her folks leave to play and none other.

A letter from Margaret Paston, 1449

SOURCE 12

The Sherborne Missal was used for the three Christmas Masses – one at midnight, one at dawn and one during the day – in Sherborne Abbey in Dorset. The midnight Mass was the most important one because the Church said that Jesus was born on the darkest hour of the darkest day. Candles are still lit at midnight as a sign that Jesus (the light) has brought hope to a sick and sinful world (the dark). This robin was drawn in a margin of the Missal.

In the sixteenth century, a man called John Stow tried to find out about Christmas in earlier times. He said he read a description, written in 1444, of:

SOURCE 14

A tree being set up in the midst of the pavement in Cornhill in London, fast [firm] in the ground, nailed full of holme [holly] and ivy for the disport [enjoyment] of the people at Christmas . . . Every man's house was decked with holme, ivy, bayes and whatsoever the season of the year afforded to be green.

John Stow

activity

I Here is a list of things that go with Christmas:

Father Christmas	midnight mass	decorations	candles
Christmas cards	nativity plays	mistletoe	carols
Christmas trees	family games	presents	

a Use the information in this section and sources 11–14 to work out (i) which of them were part of the medieval Christmas, (ii) how and when each of these came to be associated with Christmas.
b Find out how and when the other things came to be associated with Christmas.
c Which of the things on your list come from Christianity and which do not?

assignments

I Find out which festivals and holy days were celebrated in the Middle Ages.
a Make a calendar to show when they came in the year.
b Find out in detail what happened in two of them that are not described in this book. Use words and drawings to describe them yourself.

2 Make a chart or display to show all the ways in which Christmas has changed since it started.

3 In what ways was the medieval Christmas the same as ours and in what ways was it different?

Monks, nuns and friars

Many men and women chose to live a religious life by becoming a monk or a nun and living in a monastery or convent. They had to make vows, or promises, to follow the rules. Three of the most important were the vows of obedience (to obey the abbot or abbess in charge of the monastery), of poverty (to own no possessions) and of chastity (to have no sexual relations).

People who went into monasteries had their hair cut in a special way to show that they were living apart from the rest of the world and were devoting themselves to God.

SOURCE 15

A man about to join a monastery has his hair cut.

For poorer people monasteries offered a secure home as well as a chance to live a religous life. For some women, becoming a nun gave them the chance of a career. There were many famous and important abbesses.

Sometimes parents decided to send a child off to become a monk or nun. That happened to Orderic Vitalis. This is how he told the story as he looked back on it more than fifty years later:

SOURCE 16

. . . when I was five years old I was put to school in the town of Shrewsbury . . . There Siward, an illustrious priest, taught me my letters for five years, and instructed me in psalms and hymns. Then, O glorious God, you inspired my father to put me under your rule. So, weeping, he gave me, a weeping child, into the care of the monk Reginald, and sent me away for love of you and never saw me again. And I . . . obeyed him willingly . . . for he promised me in your name that if I became a monk I should go to Heaven after my death.

And so, a boy of ten, I crossed the English Channel and came into Normandy, unknown to all, knowing no one. There I heard a language that I did not understand . . . But I found nothing but kindness and friendship among strangers. I was received as a monk in the abbey of Saint-Evroul by the venerable Abbot Mainer . . . I have lived as a monk in that abbey for fifty-six years, and have been loved and honoured by my fellow monks far more than I have deserved.

Orderic Vitalis, *History of the Church*, 1141

SOURCE 17

Property owned by St Mary's, York.

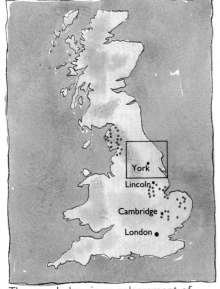

The map below is an enlargement of the area in the box.

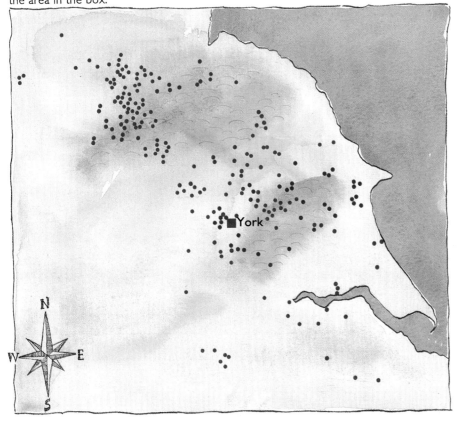

There were different kinds, or orders, of monks and nuns in the Middle Ages. Each order had monasteries all over Europe. Monks and nuns served God by cutting themselves off from everyday life. Friars did the opposite. They lived among ordinary people, often travelling around preaching and teaching about Christianity.

SOURCE 18

Nuns in chapel.

SOURCE 19

Religious orders in Britain.

Monks and Nuns	Friars
The Benedictines **Founded:** 525 by St Benedict in Italy. **Arrived in Britain:** 597, led by St Augustine who founded a monastery at Canterbury and became first Archbishop of Canterbury. **Information:** The first order of monks to be founded. Followed a set of instructions drawn up by Benedict, known as Benedict's 'Rule' which included the vows of poverty, obedience and chastity and the rule that all monks should work with their hands as well as attend services and pray. Wore a black habit (tunic) and cowl (hood) over a white gown. Sometimes called 'Black Monks'.	**The Franciscans** **Founded:** 1209, by St Francis of Assisi in Italy. **Arrived in Britain:** 1224. **Information:** Francis was the son of a rich Italian cloth merchant. He decided to live as Christ had done, without a home or possessions, and travelled in Italy preaching to poor people and looking after the sick in return for food. Many followers joined him. The order spread throughout Europe and as far as China (1245). Francis also founded a convent for his friend and follower St Clare, where she set up the Franciscan order of nuns, the Poor Clares.
The Cluniacs **Founded:** 910, when Duke William of Aquitaine gave land for a new monastery at Cluny in France. **Arrived in Britain:** 1077. First monastery built at Lewes, Sussex. **Information:** Followed Benedict's Rule, but made some changes to it and spent much more time in prayer and services. Dress – very like the Benedictines.	
The Cistercians **Founded:** 1098, by St Robert de Champagne at Citeaux in France. **Arrived in Britain:** 1131. First monastery built at Rievaulx, Yorkshire. **Information:** Founded to follow a stricter form of Benedict's Rule. St Bernard was their most famous founder member and teacher. Very skilled at farming. Made their habits out of grey-white sheep's wool, so known as the 'White Monks'.	**The Dominicans** **Founded:** 1216, by St Dominic in Spain. **Arrived in Britain:** 1221. **Information:** Dominic was a Spanish noble who trained for the Church and went to university. Inspired by the ideas of Francis he decided to try to preach to and teach ordinary people so that they really understood about Christianity. Dominicans were usually better educated than most priests and very good teachers.
The Carthusians **Founded:** 1084, by St Bruno at Chartreuse in France. **Arrived in Britain:** about 1178. First monastery built at Witham, Essex. **Information:** Lived in almost unbroken silence. Ate one vegetarian meal a day. Wore a white gown and cowl. A piece of cloth went over the gown and hung down front and back.	

SOURCE 20

A friar preaching from an open-air pulpit.

activity

1 What evidence is there in source 17 that monasteries could be wealthy? What do you think could be the dangers for a monastery that became wealthy?

2 What does source 22 tell you about the problems and difficulties of trying to lead a religious life as a nun or monk?

SOURCE 21

Looking after the sick.

The monks and nuns were supposed to strictly follow the rules and keep their vows. However, there is evidence that they did not always do this:

SOURCE 22

We have convinced ourselves by clear proof that some nuns of your house bring with them to church, birds, rabbits, hounds and such like things ... and give more heed [thought] to them than to the services of the church ... to the grievous peril [danger] of their souls.

Letter from the Bishop of Winchester to the Abbess of Romsey, 1387

assignments

1a Make a list of all the different tasks carried out by monks, nuns and friars. Use the information in this section and in sources 18–21. Also look back to Part 1, sources 10, 11 and activity 2.
b Which of these tasks are carried out by other people today?
c How important do you think monks, nuns and friars were as members of medieval society? Explain your reasons carefully.

2 We have very little information about what ordinary people in the Middle Ages really believed. Most of the sources are pictures that tell us what they were supposed to believe.
a Look at all the sources in Part 5 so far. How many can you find like that?
b What kind of sources do you think would be useful for telling us more about what ordinary people believed?
c Why do you think they are so hard to find?

The Church and the King: the case of Thomas Becket and Henry II

English kings often quarrelled with the Pope and the Archbishop of Canterbury. The problem was that the Pope wanted to be in charge of everything that went on in the Church, but the king wanted to be in charge of everything that went on in his own kingdom, including some things to do with the Church. When the Archbishop of Canterbury died in 1162, Henry II wanted someone he could trust as the new archbishop, someone who would be on his side.

Henry's Chancellor, Thomas Becket, lived and worked very closely with the king. He advised him about matters of government and helped him to make decisions. They spent a lot of time hunting together and they became close friends.

Henry came up with a brilliant idea. He would persuade the bishops to choose Thomas Becket as their new archbishop. He knew he could rely on Thomas. Thomas was not a priest and if he became archbishop he would have to become one. At first he refused, but in the end he gave way.

Sources 23 and 24 come from **William fitz Stephen's** *Life of Thomas, Archbishop of Canterbury and Martyr* which was written shortly after 1170. They describe Thomas before and after he became archbishop:

SOURCE 23

Thomas was handsome, tall ... with a sharp intelligence. He was high spirited. He took pity on the poor ... and disliked proud people. He was polite and kind.

When he was chancellor, he threw his house open to all men of whatever rank who came to the king's court and were in need of hospitality. His table shone with gold and silver cups and bowls full of dainty dishes and precious wines.

William fitz Stephen, *Life of Thomas*, c. 1171

SOURCE 24

He wore a hair shirt of the roughest kind which reached to his knees and swarmed with lice and his usual drink was water ... Immediately over his hair-shirt he wore the habit [clothes] of a monk as he was the abbot of the monks of Canterbury.

i **William fitz Stephen** wrote at the beginning of his life of Thomas Becket, 'I was the fellow-citizen of Thomas, his chaplain and a member of his household. When he sat to hear cases, I was the reader of the letters and documents put forward. I was a witness of his murder in Canterbury, and many other things which are here written I saw with my eyes and heard with my ears; others I learnt from those who knew of them.'

activity

la What do sources 23 and 24 tell you about Thomas as a person?

b How did Thomas change once he became archbishop?

c Do you think Henry expected this change? Give your reasons.

2a William fitz Stephen knew Thomas well. What words and phrases in these sources tell you that he also liked and admired him?

b Read the information about William fitz Stephen. How accurate do you think his information about Thomas is likely to be? Give your reasons for your answer.

He entertained the outcast and needy in his house and he clothed many against the severe cold of winter.

The glorious Archbishop Thomas, against the expectations of the king and everyone else, so suddenly experienced conversion to God that all men were astonished at it.

William fitz Stephen, *Life of Thomas*, c.1171

i **Roger of Pontigny** *was a monk at the abbey of Pontigny in France. Becket spent two years of his exile there and Roger was his personal servant. A monk of Pontigny wrote a Life of Becket in about 1176. Some historians are not sure that it was Roger himself who wrote it, but others think that he did.*

The quarrel

SOURCE 25

This picture comes from the only medieval illustrated book about Thomas Becket. It was drawn in about 1235 and shows Becket riding away from Henry.

The Church in England had its own law courts. Priests and anyone who worked for the Church could claim 'benefit of clergy' if they were accused of a crime. This meant they could only be tried in one of the church courts and the punishments there were usually much less harsh than in the king's courts. Henry wanted to stop this custom, but Becket refused. A French monk called **Roger of Pontigny** described how Henry and Becket met in a field outside Northampton in 1163 to try to sort out their differences:

SOURCE 26

The king then said to the archbishop, 'Have I not raised you from a poor and lowly station [position] to the pinnacle [very top] of honour and rank? How is it then that so many proofs of my love for you have so soon been obliterated [wiped out] from your mind, that you are not only ungrateful, but oppose me in everything?'

The archbishop replied, 'Far be it from me to show myself ungrateful or to act against your will in anything, so long as it agrees with the will of God. For kings should be obeyed, yet not against God. As St Peter wrote, "We ought to obey God rather than men".'

Roger of Pontigny, *Life of Becket*, 1176

activity

3a Why was Henry angry with Thomas in source?
b What was Thomas's argument in reply?
c The argument was about who had the most authority – that is the most right to be obeyed. Do you think either of them had right on their side? In what way?
4 Roger of Pontigny was not at Northampton.
a How do you think he found out what happened?
b How reliable do you think his account is?

Becket in exile

Becket refused to do what Henry wanted and resign as archbishop, but in 1164 he was forced to escape to France where he stayed in exile until 1170. While he was there a French bishop, Arnulf of Lisieux, wrote to him about Henry:

SOURCE 28

You have to deal with someone whose cunning and power are feared, who is easily angered by disobedience and who takes instant revenge. He will sometimes be persuaded by humility [humbleness] and patience but he will never be forced to do something. Whatever he does openly must appear to have sprung from his own will and not from weakness. He is a great king for he stands in awe of no one and none of his subjects can resist him.

Letter from Arnulf, Bishop of Lisieux, to Thomas Becket, March 1165

In 1166 Becket wrote to Henry:

SOURCE 29

These are the words of the Archbisop of Canterbury to the King of the English . . . Since it is certain that kings receive their authority from the Church, and the Church receives hers not from kings but from Christ, so, if I may be pardoned from saying so, you have no right to give orders to bishops nor to drag priests into royal courts.

Letter from Thomas Becket to Henry II, May 1166

The murder of Becket

In 1170 Henry and Thomas Becket made up and Becket returned to Canterbury. He immediately excommunicated all the bishops who had supported the king. Several of them went straight to the king, who was in Normandy, to protest. He asked them for advice:

SOURCE 30

At length one of them said, 'My lord, while Thomas lives you will not have peace or quiet, nor see good days.' At this fury, bitterness and anger against the archbishop overcame the king and showed in his face and gestures. Seeing this, four knights of his household who were eager to win the king's favour met together and swore to arrange the archbishop's death. Then they left the court.

William fitz Stephen, *Life of Thomas Becket*

The four knights arrived in Canterbury in the afternoon of 29 December 1170. By now the king had realised that they had left his court. He suspected what they were up to and gave orders to stop them, but it was too late. They forced their way into the archbishop's palace, accused Becket of breaking the peace with the

Becket returns from exile.

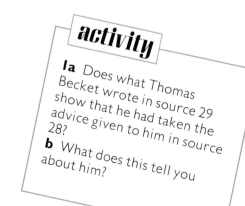

activity

1a Does what Thomas Becket wrote in source 29 show that he had taken the advice given to him in source 28?

b What does this tell you about him?

SOURCE 31

The murder of Thomas Becket. From an early thirteenth-century manuscript.

king and demanded that he should leave the country again. Becket refused angrily and the knights walked out, only to return a few minutes later in full armour with their weapons. Becket refused to run away so the monks pushed him into the cathedral. There the knights killed him on the steps of the altar.

Thomas, saint and martyr

It was reported that when the people of Canterbury heard of Thomas Becket's death, they rushed with bottles to gather up his blood, believing that it could perform miracles. His tomb in Canterbury Cathedral became the most popular shrine in England. Pilgrims reported every sort of miracle: mad people became sane, blind people could see, people with leprosy were cured. In 1173 the Pope declared Thomas, 'God's holy martyr', a saint.

When Henry heard of the murder he cried out loudly, saying he had neither wanted it to happen nor known that it would. In 1174 he walked barefoot through Canterbury to Becket's tomb where bishops whipped his back. In that way one of Europe's proudest and strongest rulers showed his sorrow and repentance in public, and so ended the ten year quarrel with the Church.

assignments

la Write down three things that helped to cause the murder of Thomas Becket (three causes) and three things that happened because of it (three results).
b From these choose the cause and the result that you think were the most important and write a few sentences to say why you think so.

2 Imagine you are a judge who has been asked to decide who was most responsible for the death of Thomas Becket. You can choose between Henry, Becket himself, the bishops and the knights. Write a report about how much each was to blame. Then give your judgement, with reasons, about who was most to blame.

3 Look back at sources 7, 10 and 16.
a What do they tell you about the things people believed in the Middle Ages?
b There are several different types of sources here. What are they?
c Have you found some types more useful than others in finding out about what people believed?

4a Make a list of all the reasons why you think the Middle Ages have been called an 'Age of Faith' and write a paragraph about each one.
b Do you think 'Age of Faith' is a good name for the Middle Ages? Explain your reasons for your answer.
c Choose what you think is a good name to describe the times we live in and explain why you have chosen it.

The British Isles in the twelfth century

SOURCE 1

Ireland in 1120

Gaelic the common language. No common ruler. There were several Irish kingdoms, and the Norse king of Dublin had the king of Norway as his overlord. Everyone Christian, including those in the Norse area.

Scotland in 1120

No common language – Gaelic, Norse and English all spoken north of the line from the River Tweed to the Solway. 'Scotia', the land of the Scots, meant the land north of the River Forth, but the Scottish king was now based in the English-speaking Lothian area.

One Scottish king, but he was barely obeyed in Galloway, Moray, Argyll and Caithness, and not at all in the Western Isles which belonged to Norway. Everyone Christian.

The Church in 1120

The Pope in Rome was the overall head of the Church in all countries of the British Isles. The Archbishop of York claimed to have authority over bishops in Scotland where there was no archbishop. The Archbishop of Canterbury claimed to have authority over the Archbishop of York and also over bishops in Wales and Ireland.

England in 1120

English the common language of the English people, but the Norman barons and churchmen spoke French. There were also different versions, or dialects, of English spoken in different areas.

One king, who was also Duke of Normandy. Everyone Christian.

Wales in 1120

Celtic the common language. The Celtic word for Wales, 'Cymry', meant 'people of one region', but the Welsh lived under several leaders and none called themself king or prince of Wales. Everyone Christian.

KEY

/// area of Ireland and Wales occupied by Norman (English) barons by about 1200

▨ 1139–57 occupied by Scotland

Map labels: N E S W · ORKNEY AND SHETLAND · WESTERN ISLES · CAITHNESS · ARGYLL · MORAY · SCOTLAND · R. Forth · LOTHIAN · ← border 1157 · R. Tweed · GALLOWAY · Solway Firth · MAN · R. Tees · IRELAND · ULSTER · CONNAUGHT · MEATH · R. Shannon · Dublin · LEINSTER · MUNSTER · Waterford · Wexford · WALES · GWYNEDD · POWYS · CEREDIGION · DYFED · DEHEUBARTH · GWENT · R. Severn · Bristol Channel · York · ENGLAND · Huntingdon · London · R. Thames · Canterbury

Gruffydd ap Cynan

Gruffydd was born in Dublin. His mother was part Gaelic and part Norse and was supposed to be related to Rollo, William I's ancestor. Gruffydd often sailed back to Dublin or Leinster, either to hide from his enemies in Wales or raise soldiers to fight them.

In 1098 the fleet of King Magnus of Norway sailed into the Irish Sea. Magnus came to deal with trouble in the southern most part of his realm, the Norse kingdom of Dublin. Magnus quickly regained control and helped Gruffydd stop the Norman barons who William I and William II of England had encouraged to extend their lands along the south Wales coast. Then Magnus sailed home.

activity

Look at source I and the information in the text.
1a What evidence is there that around 1120 England, Scotland, Wales and Ireland (i) were not separate individual countries in their own right and (ii) were influenced by rulers outside the British Isles.
b Which rulers were these?
2 Why do you think that English kings wanted to control the northern shore of the Bristol Channel?
3a Who held lands in both Scotland and England?
b What else linked Scotland and England?
c What would be the advantages of these links for Scotland?
d Can you think of any disadvantages?

Henry I, Alexander I and David I

Henry I of England wanted to make sure that barons he could trust held the lands near the border with Scotland. So he gave a lot of land near the River Tees to a Norman baron, Robert de Brus.

In 1100 Henry married Matilda, the daughter of the Scottish king. Her brother, Alexander, became the next Scottish king and served in Henry's army in Wales in 1114. Matilda's younger brother, David, lived in Henry I's court and Henry gave him lands in Yorkshire, Huntingdon, and Cherbourg (in Normandy). In 1124 he succeeded Alexander as King of the Scots. Like Henry, David I wanted barons he could trust to hold the border land. So he gave Robert de Brus land near Galloway in southern Scotland.

Wales and Scotland

Wales

| 1137–57 | The Welsh take advantage of the civil war between Stephen and Matilda to raid England. |
| 1157–65 | Henry II sends expeditions into Wales. |

Scotland

1139–57	Scots take over land in the far north of England during the civil war.
1157	Henry II drives the Scots out of the north of England.
1173	The Scots king, William the Lion, invades England.
1174	Henry captures William and forces him to promise loyalty and do homage for the throne of Scotland.
1189	William persuades King Richard I to cancel the homage in return for money.

Henry II and Ireland

1169   Rory O'Connor, King of Connacht, drives Dermot MacMurrough, King of Leinster into exile. Dermot hires English knights from south Wales to help him fight back.

1170   Baron Richard de Clare, nicknamed 'Strongbow', joins them.

1171   Strongbow captures Dublin and marries Dermot's daughter. Dermot dies. Strongbow succeeds him as King of Leinster. King Henry II of England invades Ireland.

1172   Strongbow and most Irish kings accept Henry's overlordship. Henry takes Dublin, Wexford and Waterford as royal land. Irish bishops accept the Archbishop of Canterbury as their superior.

1176   Strongbow dies and the rest of his lands pass to Henry.

SOURCE 2

When these [Strongbow's] successes had become known to the King of England, he was moved to anger against the earl for having attempted so great an enterprise, not only without consulting him but even in defiance of him, and also because the earl had taken to himself the glory of so noble a conquest, which ought rather to have been given to the king as his superior.

William of Newburgh, *The History of England*, 1197

SOURCE 3

Then the king went to Oxford, and in general council there he made his son John, king in Ireland, by the grant and confirmation of Pope Alexander. At the same council the king was attended by Rhys ap Gruffydd, sub-king of South Wales, and Dafydd ab Owain, sub-king of North Wales, who had been given the king's half-sister in marriage.

The Chronicle of Roger of Howden, 1185

activity

I Use pages 80–82 to work out what changes took place in Ireland, Scotland and Wales between 1120 and 1175.
2 Look at source 2.
a Imagine you are Henry II. You hear the news about Strongbow's success in Ireland. Make a list of the reasons why you think you should invade Ireland. What might happen if you do not?
b What was Henry II's main reason for invading Ireland?
3 What does source 3 tell you about the place of England in the British Isles in 1185?

Ireland, 1172–1500

After 1172 the Norman barons expanded their territory in wars against the native Irish lords. In 1185 Henry II made John, his younger son, King of Ireland (see source 3) and when John became King of England in 1199 the two kingships were combined. After that English kings appointed a lieutenant, or governor, to be head of the 'Lordship of Ireland'. He was responsible to the king for looking after law and order, raising taxes and meeting with the Irish Parliament which was first called in 1264.

In 1200 most barons with land in Ireland also held land in England; but by 1500 very few did. They called themselves the 'English of Ireland' and felt themselves to be different from barons in England.

The native Irish lords continued to control large areas of Ireland. They fought many battles and skirmishes along their borders with the English barons. But the two sides also got to know each other and sometimes their sons and daughters married. Even so, Irish lords were not invited to Parliament and were not appointed to any government jobs by the English kings.

SOURCE 4

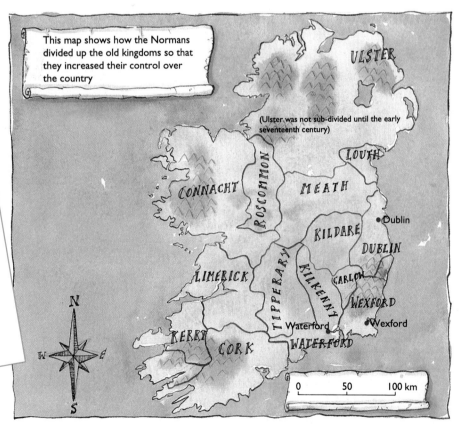

This map shows how the Normans divided up the old kingdoms so that they increased their control over the country

(Ulster was not sub-divided until the early seventeenth century)

activity

4a Use source 4 and the information above to work out the main changes in Ireland between 1172 and 1500.
b When did the king have most power in Ireland? When did he have least?
5 What do you think the Irish and English lords had in common with one another? What separated them?

Ireland in the fourteenth century.

Wales, 1200–1500

The princes of Deheubarth and Gwynedd

From about 1160 to 1191, Rhys ap Gruffydd extended the power of Deheubarth. He captured Cardigan Castle from the English and was recognised as sub-king by Henry II of England.

In 1197 Rhys ap Gruffydd died and Llywelyn ap Iorwerth, King of Gwynedd, extended his lordship over both Powys and Deheubarth, now divided between the sons of Rhys. He also, for a while, managed to control the English royal castles of Cardigan and Carmarthen.

Llywelyn called himself 'Prince of North Wales' and in 1258 his grandson, Llywelyn ap Gruffydd, first used the title 'Prince of Wales'. In 1267 Henry III recognised Llywelyn as 'Prince of Wales'.

SOURCE 5

Wales in 1300.

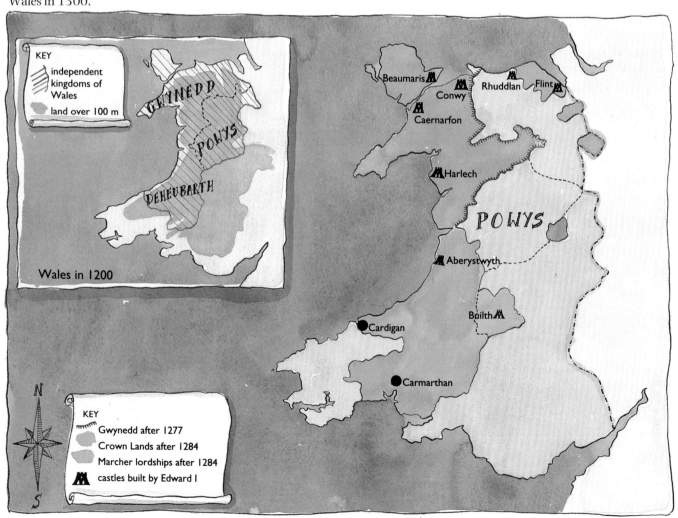

KEY

independent kingdoms of Wales

land over 100 m

Wales in 1200

GWYNEDD

POWYS

DEHEUBARTH

Beaumaris

Conwy

Caernarfon

Rhuddlan

Flint

Harlech

POWYS

Aberystwyth

Builth

Cardigan

Carmarthan

N

S

KEY

Gwynedd after 1277

Crown Lands after 1284

Marcher lordships after 1284

castles built by Edward I

SOURCE 6

Harlech Castle. This is one of the castles that Edward I built to hold down Wales after he had defeated Llywelyn.

1274 Llywelyn ap Gruffydd refused to do homage to the new English king, Edward I.

1277 Edward I invaded Wales and defeated Llywelyn. The Treaty of Aberconwy (Conway) allowed Llywelyn to keep his title but restricted his rule to Gwynedd itself.

1282 Llywelyn and his brother, Dafydd, led an uprising against the English. Edward I invaded Gwynedd and Llywelyn was killed.

1283 Dafydd was captured and executed. Edward started to build castles throughout the Welsh kingdoms.

1284 The Statute of Wales divided Wales into Crown Lands (divided into shires under sheriffs), areas under Welsh rulers (mainly Powys) who lost their old rights and became barons under Edward, and the Marcher lordships.

activity

1 Look at the information and make a list of all the differences in the organisation and control of Welsh lands between 1200 and 1300.
2a What do you think it was about Deheubarth and Gwynedd that made them the parts of Wales where the Welsh princes were the strongest?
b When do you think the power of (i) Deheubarth, and (ii) Gwynedd was at its greatest?
3 Edward was prepared to deal with Llywelyn in 1277, but not in 1282. What do you think changed his mind?
4 What does source 6 tell you about Edward I's determination to crush the Welsh and the amount of money he was prepared to spend?

i **Gerald of Wales** was born around 1145. He was part Norman and part Welsh. He was educated at the Abbey of St Peter in Gloucester and became Archdeacon of Brecon. In 1185 he sailed to Ireland with Prince John as his chaplain and adviser. Later he wrote two books about Ireland. In 1188 he toured Wales with the Archbishop of Canterbury and afterwards wrote The Journey Through Wales and later The Description of Wales.

i **Bard** is a Celtic word meaning a particular kind of poet whose duty to the people was to praise the deeds and lament the deaths of kings and chiefs. There were bards in Ireland and Scotland as well as Wales. They trained in special 'bardic schools'.

activity

1 What do sources 7, 8 and 11 tell you about the people of Wales in the Middle Ages?
2 According to sources 9 and 10, when did the Welsh have the best chance of getting the better of the English?
3 Use sources 8–12 to make two lists, one of all the strengths of the Welsh as fighters and one of all their weaknesses.

The people of Wales

Much of what we know about the people of Wales in the late twelfth century comes from the writings of **Gerald of Wales**:

SOURCE 7

The Welsh play three instruments, the harp, the pipe and the crwth [a stringed instrument]. When they play their instruments they charm and delight the ear with the sweetness of their music . . . They sing their traditional songs not in unison as is done elsewhere, but in parts. In their narrative poems and speeches . . . they are so inventive . . . that they produce works of art . . . Many poets in Wales, **bards** *as they call them, devote all their energies to this kind of composition.*

Gerald of Wales, *The Description of Wales*, 1194

SOURCE 8

They do not live in towns, villages or castles, but lead a solitary existence, deep in the woods . . . The whole population lives almost entirely on oats and the produce of their herds, milk, cheese and butter. They eat plenty of meat but little bread. They pay no attention to commerce, shipping or industry, and their only pre-occupation is military training. They are passionately devoted to their freedom and to the defence of their country . . . They think it a disgrace to die in bed but an honour to die in battle.

Gerald of Wales, *The Description of Wales*, 1194

The Welsh were fierce fighters, but they had their weaknesses as well as their strengths:

SOURCE 9

They may not shine in open combat and in fixed formation, but they harass the enemy by their ambushes and their night-attacks. In a single battle they are easily beaten, but they are difficult to conquer in a long war, for they are not troubled by hunger or cold, fighting does not seem to tire them, they do not lose heart when things go wrong, and after one defeat they are ready to fight again and to face once more the hazards of war.

Gerald of Wales, *The Description of Wales*, 1194

SOURCE 10

The Welsh, despite their frequent victories over their opponents, weighing future events in their minds and taking counsel among themselves, said, 'We know that the kingdom of England is in a very disturbed state, but when peace is established we shall not be able to resist them, as they will unite in falling on us.'

Matthew Paris, *Greater Chronicle*, 1258–59

SOURCE 11

A Welsh spearman.

SOURCE 12

The English are striving for power, the Welsh for freedom; the English are fighting for material gain, the Welsh to avoid a disaster; the English soldiers are hired mercenaries, the Welsh are defending their homeland.

Gerald of Wales, *The Description of Wales*, 1194

Owain Glyn Dwr

Many Welsh people resented English rule after the conquests of Edward I; but it was too strong for them to be able to do much about it. In 1400 a landholder in Powys, called Owain Glyn Dwr, led the last great Welsh uprising of the Middle Ages. He had studied law in London and served in Richard II's army.

When King Henry IV supported an English lord who had wrongfully accused him of treason, Glyn Dwr led a Welsh rebellion. By 1403 he had managed to gain control of most of the country. He declared himself 'Prince of Wales' and appealed to the Irish and the Scots to join in a Celtic alliance against the English. His vision was an independent Wales. He called a Welsh parliament and he planned to found two universities.

Gradually the king regained control of Wales, though he never defeated Glyn Dwr in pitched battle. Glyn Dwr's supporters drifted away and by 1410 he was a fugitive on the run. Later he refused a free pardon and died in hiding.

assignments

1a Use the sources and information in Part Six to work out what you think the Welsh were fighting for in their struggle against the English.
b Either give a talk, or make a display of words and pictures, to explain your ideas.

2a Make a list of the reasons why you think Llywelyn ap Gruffydd failed to keep his independence from the English.
b Use the information and sources in Part 6 to work out what you think he should have done instead.
c Write him a letter of advice.

Scotland

After 1200 Scottish kings began to increase their power. In 1202 King William IV forced the Norwegian Earl of Caithness to swear loyalty to him. The line of the English/Scottish border was agreed by treaty in 1237. In 1266 the king of Norway gave the Isle of Man and the Western Isles to Alexander III.

Scottish kings were not crowned by a bishop like English kings. Instead the Scottish nobles enthroned their kings on a special stone in an open air ceremony at Scone near Perth.

SOURCE 13

The seal of Alexander III of Scotland.

SOURCE 14

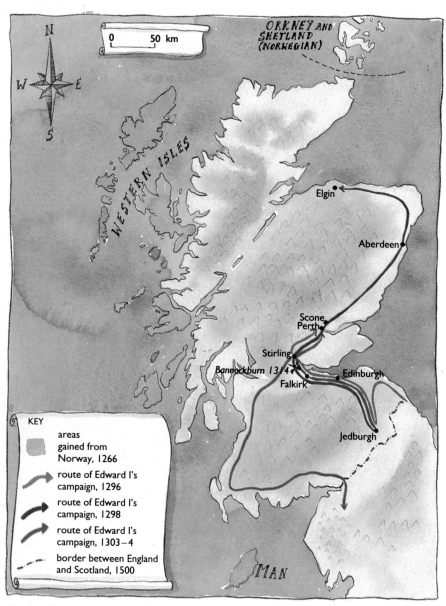

Scotland 1286–1500.

KEY

- areas gained from Norway, 1266
- route of Edward I's campaign, 1296
- route of Edward I's campaign, 1298
- route of Edward I's campaign, 1303–4
- border between England and Scotland, 1500

SOURCE 15

The English coronation chair in Westminster Abbey. Under the seat is the Stone of Scone taken by Edward I.

activity

1 What evidence is there in sources 14 and 17 that the Scots became stronger and more united after 1305?

SOURCE 16

Edward III and David II of Scotland. From a late 14th-century Book of Statutes.

Alexander III died in 1286, leaving his young granddaughter as heir, but she died soon after. The barons and bishops who were left to rule invited Edward I to decide who, of more than twelve contenders, should be king. He agreed on condition that the contenders would accept him as their overlord. This they did, and Edward selected John Baliol to be the new king.

The barons were annoyed that John had to swear loyalty to Edward. They persuaded him to get rid of his English advisers and to make a treaty with the king of France, Edward's enemy. Edward was furious. He marched north, deposed John and took the Stone of Scone back with him to England.

Edward had to lead an army into Scotland twice more against rebels who were now led by William Wallace. In 1305 Wallace was executed and the Scots chose Robert the Bruce as their new king.

Robert also fought against English rule and in 1314 led the Scots to victory over Edward II at Bannockburn. The fighting continued, however, and in 1320 the Scottish barons and the 'whole community of the realm of Scotland' sent a letter called *The Declaration of Arbroath* to the Pope, asking him to tell King Edward II of England to leave them in peace:

SOURCE 17

'For, as long as a hundred of us remain alive, we will never . . . be subjected to the lordship of the English.'

From the Declaration of Arbroath, 1320.

In 1328, after further fighting, Edward III recognised Robert as King of Scots and Scotland as independent. For most of his reign Edward III was occupied by the war with France which became known as the Hundred Years War. The Scots continued their alliance with the French and continued to dispute land on the border with the English. At one point Edward III and David II discussed the idea of uniting the two kingdoms; but feeling in Scotland was strongly against this. By 1500 Scotland was still firmly independent.

assignments

1a Make a list of the ways in which the power of the Scottish kings grew between 1200 and 1328 and write a few sentences to describe each one.
b Was the change in their power rapid or gradual?

2 Use sources 14 and 17 and the information in the text to work out three reasons why you think Edward III eventually recognised Scotland as independent. Explain why you have chosen each one.

7
Chivalry and Warfare

War was as common as peace in the middle ages.

SOURCE 1

1066–1070: Norman Conquest of England.
1101–1119: Norman barons supported by French king rebel against Henry I .
1139–1154: Civil wars between Stephen and Matilida.
1166–1171 } Wars against the Irish.
1185
1173–1174: Rebellion of Henry II 's sons.
1189–1192: Richard I on the Third Cursade.
1194–1199: Richard I defends Normandy against the French.
1209–1211: John campaigns in Scotland, Ireland and Wales.
1213–1217: War against French.
1215–1216: Civil war between John and barons.
1228–1231: Henry III leads unsuccessful expeditions against the French and Welsh.
1258–1267: Barons rebel against Henry III .
1272–1277: Welsh raids. Edward I invades Wales.
1282–1283: Edward I defeats Welsh.
1296–1298 } Edward I campaigns in Scotland.
1304–1305
1293–1297: War against French.
1337–1375 } The Hundred Years War with France.
1411–1453
1399–1408: Uprisings against Henry IV who had deposed Richard II .
1455–1464
1469–1471 } The Wars of the Roses (civil war).
1483–1487

There were also many other smaller wars, campaigns and rebellions.

Wars that involved the English between 1066 and 1500.

---

activity

I This is the start of a bar graph based on the information in source 1. The first column shows the number of years between 1066 and 1500 when there was a war going on.
a Copy the graph and then use the information in source 1 to add a second column showing the number of years when there were no wars.
b Make a second bar graph to show (i) the number of years which the English spent fighting civil wars, (ii) the number of years they spent fighting the Irish, Welsh and Scots, and (iii) the number of years they spent fighting abroad.

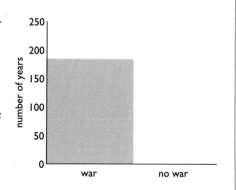

Since war was so common, men were often away. Source **3** shows Sir Geoffrey Luttrell leaving home. While the men were away, women had to look after their affairs and run the manor:

SOURCE 2

Because that knights, squires and gentlemen go upon journeys and follow the wars, it beseemeth [is the duty of] wives to be wise in all they do, for that most often they dwell at home without their husbands who are at court or in divers [various] lands.

Christine de Pisan, *The Book of the Three Virtues*, 1406

ℹ Christine de Pisan was French and the first woman known to have earned her living entirely as a writer. She married before she was fifteen and when she was twenty-five her husband died leaving her to bring up three young children on her own. Two of her most famous books were The City of Women (1405), which contained stories to show the virtues of women, and The Book of the Three Virtues (1406), which was about the duties of women in the different ranks of society.

SOURCE 3

Sir Geoffrey Luttrell being seen off by his wife and daughter-in-law. From the *Luttrell Psalter*, 1342.

Knighthood and Chivalry

From 1066 when the Normans first introduced them into England a successful English army depended on its armoured knights on horse-back.

A king had to have knights in his army just as a modern general has to have tanks. Knights could easily destroy every kind of opponent, except other knights; they could move fast through the countryside; they could attack or retreat quickly. The problem was that they were expensive. Their armour and equipment cost a lot; their horses had to be a special breed that could move quickly while carrying a heavy weight; and the knights themselves had to have a long training to learn the difficult fighting skills that they needed.

SOURCE 4

A knight. This was drawn in about 1138 in Normandy. Find:
- his armour and shield
- his spear. The knight's skill was to get his own and his horse's weight exactly behind the point of his spear as it struck his opponent, but without falling off his own horse
- the high saddle. What do you think it was for?
- the stirrups. These first appeared in Europe in the eighth century.

Why do you think it would have been impossible to have armoured knights on horse-back before stirrups were invented?

i **Chivalry** The English word in the Middle Ages was 'chivalrie' which came from the French word 'chevalerie' which meant 'horsemanship' and 'knighthood', and came in turn from the French word 'cheval' meaning 'a horse'. Later on, when people looked back to the Middle Ages from the eighteenth century, they started to use the word 'chivalry' to describe the qualities that made an ideal knight; and they talked of the Middle Ages as the 'Age of Chivalry'.

That was one reason why a king like William I gave out land to his barons. In return they had to provide a certain number of knights for his army. The barons then gave land to their knights so that they would be able to afford to buy and look after their horses and equipment, to train, and to pass on their skills to the young men whose ambition was to be a knight too.

SOURCE 5

A Crusader knight in the thirteenth century.

SOURCE 6

The tomb of William Marshal.

Source 6 shows William Marshal portrayed on his tomb in the Temple Church, London. When he died in 1219, people thought of him as an example of an ideal knight. He had been a very brave and skilful fighter; he had been loyal to the kings he had served – Henry II, John and Henry III; and he had been courteous – that is, polite and considerate – in the way he treated others.

In the Middle Ages people used the word '**chivalry**' to describe the position of being a knight and all the things that were expected of knights.

This definition of what was expected of a knight was written in the late twelfth century:

SOURCE 8

What is the function [use] of orderly knighthood? To protect the church, to fight against treachery, to fend off injustice from the poor, to make peace in your own province, to shed your blood for your bretheren, and, if needs must, to lay down your life.

John of Salisbury, Policraticus, 1159–60

SOURCE 7

Sir Gilbert de Clare shown in a fourteenth-century stained-glass window in Tewkesbury Abbey, Gloucestershire.

activity

I Which picture out of sources 4, 5 and 7 do you think most fits John of Salisbury's definition? Explain your reasons.

Squires

Barons and knights started to train their sons to follow in their footsteps when they were still very young. They usually sent them to live in the household of another lord who agreed to teach them the ways of knighthood. To start with the boy had to serve as a page and learn how to behave to noble lords and ladies. As a teenager he became a squire and at that point he began to learn fighting skills as well.

SOURCE 9

When you enter your lord's place say 'God speed' and salute all there. Hold up your head and kneel on one knee to listen to your lord. If any speak to you, look straight at them and listen well. Answer sensibly and shortly. Stand till you are told to sit down, keep your hands and feet quiet and don't scratch yourself. Bow to your lord when you answer him. Be always ready to serve at the proper times, to bring drink, hold lights or anything else. When your lord is ready for dinner, pour out water and hold the towel till he has finished. Stand by your lord till he tells you to sit.

Cut your bread, don't break it. Don't lean on the table or dirty the cloth, or hang your head over your dish or eat with a full mouth. Don't dip your meat in the salt-cellar or put your knife in your mouth or make a noise eating. When the meal is over, clean your knives and put them in their places, rise without laughing and joking and go to your lord's table and stand there till grace is said.

From a book of instructions telling pages how to behave

SOURCE 10

A page slicing bread on bended knee.

This description of a squire comes from a poem called *The Canterbury Tales*:

SOURCE 11 ·

Embroidered was his tunic, like a mead [meadow]
Covered with springing flowers white and red.
Singing he was or fluting all the day.
He was as fresh as is the month of May.
Short was his gown, with sleeves both long and
*   wide.*
Well could he sit his horse and fairly ride . . .
Courteous he was, modest in mein [appearance] and
*   able,*
And carved before his father at the table.

Geoffrey Chaucer, *The Canterbury Tales*, Prologue, c. 1387

activity

I Use sources 9–11 to work out what pages and squires had to learn. You can find out about two different kinds of things:

a Skills
Skills are things you can do such as boiling an egg or riding a bike.
Here are the beginnings of two lists, one for pages and one for squires, of the skills they had to have. Copy them and then add as many things as you can find to each one.

Pages
Hold a towel
Stand still

Squires
Carve meat
Sing

b Manners
Manners are polite ways of behaving. Pages and squires had to learn good manners. Use the sources to add to these lists:

Good manners
Cutting bread

Bad manners
Breaking bread

SOURCE 12

A knight and his lady. A shield painted in the 15th century.

> **i** **Troubadour**   A troubadour was both a poet and a musician who usually came from southern France. Troubadours were often of noble birth and they sang poems about their favourite subjects: courtly love, war and nature.

Courtly Love

The squire probably found himself among many other young men – knights, squires and servants – in his lord's household and they usually outnumbered the women – the lord's wife, their daughters and servants – by a long way. Squires probably often found themselves in love. But there was no question of getting married unless their parents arranged it; and they never did that until they found a girl whose parents had money.

It became fashionable for knights to choose a married lady and love her from a distance without her knowing. The knight fought for her in battles and tournaments. He wrote poems about her. This became known as 'Courtly Love'. Why do you think it happened?

SOURCE 13

Alas! I thought I knew so much about love, and I know so little! For I cannot help loving her from whom I will gain nothing. She has taken my heart, and taken myself, and her own self and all the world, and when she took herself from me, she left me only desire and a yearning heart.

From a **troubadour**'s song.

---

activity

2 Look at sources 12 and 13. They both tell of a knight and his lady. Find the clues in each source that:
a tell you what the knight thinks of his lady;
b tell you what the lady thinks of the knight or squire.
Make a list of the information they give you.

Tournaments

As well as learning to ride and fight on horseback, the squire got his military training by accompanying his lord to tournaments and eventually to war. Tournaments involved two teams of knights fighting each other. The only difference between tournaments and real battles was that the knight's aim in a tournament was to take his opponents prisoner rather than to kill them.

A captured knight had to give his horse and armour to his captor and sometimes a ransom too. William Marshal was famous for the fact that he had made himself a fortune through his successes in tournaments. The kings of England, apart from Edward III, did not encourage tournaments even though they were popular in France. In any case, by the fourteenth century the mock battle was being replaced by two men fighting in single combat, or 'jousting'.

SOURCE 14a

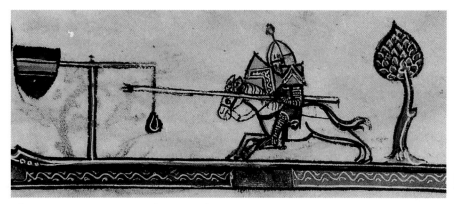

Tilting at a quintain (target).

SOURCE 14b

Preparing to joust in the fifteenth century.
What evidence is there that this is an important social occasion?

Finally, the great day came when the squire was dubbed a knight by his lord. Look at source 15 and find the shield and banner. Every knight had a design called a coat of arms, so that he could be recognised in battle.

SOURCE 15

A squire being dubbed a knight by his king.

Warfare

SOURCE 16

Attacking a city, about 1250.

SOURCE 17

The battle of Poitiers, 1356.

i **Gunpowder and cannon**
The Chinese invented gunpowder in the ninth century, using saltpetre, sulphur and crushed charcoal, and also firearms, possibly as early as the eleventh century. The first cannon were used in Europe around 1319 and in England in 1327. However, guns did not become really important until the fifteenth century, following the invention of a new type of gunpowder in 1420 which exploded properly every time it was lit.

activity

3 Use source 28 in Part I and sources 16, 17 and 18 here to make a list of all the ways in which warfare changed between 1066 and 1500. Notice in particular the kinds of soldiers and types of weapons and armour used. Did anything stay the same?

SOURCE 18

Besieging a city, late fifteenth century.

One of the big changes that had taken place by the time of the Hundred Years War (1337–1453) was that barons no longer provided the king just with mounted knights. They also recruited archers and other foot-soldiers. And instead of knights and ordinary people having to go to fight because they owed it to their lord as a feudal duty, the king paid them all wages from his Treasury.

The archers used a new and deadly weapon called a longbow. It was between one-and-a-half and two metres high and it could shoot an iron-tipped arrow through chain mail. Longbows were very important:

activity

la What evidence is there in sources 19 and 20 that the king thought that longbows were very important?
b Why do you think this was? Think about the difference the longbow made to (i) mounted knights, and (ii) the way battles were fought? (Source 17 will help you).

SOURCE 19

Again in this year it was advised and decreed that, throughout the realms of England, no man should use any play or pastime save only the longbow and arrows, on pain of death; and that every bowyer [bow-maker] and fletcher [arrow-maker] should be made quit of all his debts.

Jean Froissart, *Chronicle*, 1337

SOURCE 20

Longbow practice. From the *Luttrell Psalter*, 1342.

SOURCE 21

Looting.

SOURCE 22

A battle
outside the
city walls.

assignments

I Here are three inventions that changed the way wars were fought in the Middle Ages: the stirrup; the longbow; gunpowder.
a Explain what difference each one made.
b Which one do you think made the greatest difference?

2 You have been making lists of the manners, skills and personal qualities that you think a squire had to have in order to be a successful knight. Use these lists to make an illustrated handbook for squires called, 'Everything you need to know about being a knight'.

3a List the incidents in sources 21 and 22 that support the view that warfare in the Middle Ages was harsh and brutal, and not romantic and chivalrous.
b What evidence is there in Part 7 that the costume and ceremony of chivalry became more elaborate?
c Does that mean that knights became (i) more chivalrous, or (ii) less chivalrous?
d Look at source 7 in Part 2. (i) What evidence is there that many knights did not live up to the ideals of knighthood? (ii) Does that mean that those ideals were worthless?

8 The Beginnings of Freedom

In 1381 thousands of peasants from Kent led by Wat Tyler marched on London where they joined up with thousands more peasants from Essex and demanded to see the king. The king was Richard II and he was just fourteen years old.

SOURCE 1

Richard II trying to talk to the peasants at Rotherhithe.

Source 1 shows Richard's first attempt to talk to the peasants. He was rowed in a barge down to Rotherhithe where the men from Kent had camped. But when his attendants saw the numbers of armed peasants lining the banks they refused to let him land.

The barge pulled away followed by shouts of anger and disappointment from the crowd. Plenty of the peasants held long-bows; but no one took a shot.

A few hours later they entered London and took over the city for three days. When Wat Tyler eventually did meet King Richard, he told him what the peasants wanted:

SOURCE 2

We will that you make us free for ever, ourselves, our heirs and our lands, and that we be called 'serf' no more.

Jean Froissart, *Chronicle*

activity

1 Look back to John of Worcester's pictures of Henry I's nightmare (source 2, page 24). He imagined the king dreaming of the three orders of society, the peasants, the priests and the knights, each rising up in turn to threaten him and complain.
a Which order of society did Henry I and his successors have the most cause to fear and which the least? Explain your reasons.
b What do you think the lords of the manor must have felt when they heard about the Peasants' Revolt?
2 Compare John of Worcester's picture of the peasants with the one in source 1.
a Source 1 shows the peasants as well-armed and wearing armour. Do you think that is likely to be true?
b Why do you think the artist might have shown them like that?

However, Wat Tyler was killed and the rebellion ended. It became known as the 'Peasants' Revolt'.

As you have already learnt, peasants had to obey the lord of the manor whose land they farmed. A lot must have changed for them to feel strong enough to ask the king to make them free. What had changed? What had made their lives different?

Thirty-three years before the Peasants' Revolt something had happened which affected thousands of ordinary people. It was the worst disaster of the Middle Ages. They called it the 'Black Death'.

The Black Death

activity

3 Look at source 3. How does the artist show that the plague struck every sort of person?

SOURCE 3

The plague strikes. This fourteenth-century picture of the wall of a French church shows the plague as a blind-folded figure with arrows.

The Black Death was what is known today as 'bubonic plague'. Between 1347 and 1349 it killed about one out of every three people living in Europe. It was the most frightening thing to happen to people in the Middle Ages. They could see it coming, but did not know what to do to avoid it. No one knew what caused it. It killed every sort of person, rich and poor alike.

The disease reached Britain around the beginning of August 1348. The first people to die of it lived in seaport towns in Dorset. By 1349 it had spread throughout the country.

An Italian poet called Boccaccio who survived the plague later wrote this description of the symptoms in **The Decameron**:

SOURCE 4

In men and women alike it first showed itself by the appearance of swellings in the groin or armpits. Some grew as large as an apple or an egg. From these two parts of the body this deadly swelling soon began to spread in all directions. Then black spots began to appear on the arms or thigh.

Boccaccio, *Introduction to The Decameron*, 1351

The plague passed rapidly from person to person and place to place. Someone could be feeling well in the morning and be dead by

> **i** **The Decameron**
> *Boccaccio lived in Florence and saw what happened when the Black Death struck the town in 1348. He survived and between 1349 and 1351 he wrote a book, called* The Decameron, *about a group of ten wealthy young men and women who left Florence to live in the country and told each other stories until the plague was over. He made this up, but at the start of the book he described what it was really like in Florence during the Black Death.*

SOURCE 5

The spread of the Black Death.

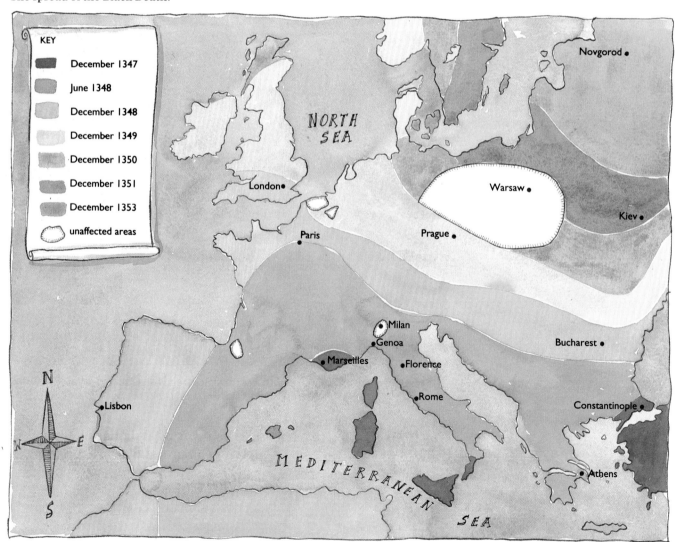

KEY

- December 1347
- June 1348
- December 1348
- December 1349
- December 1350
- December 1351
- December 1353
- unaffected areas

midday. Few people who caught it lived for more than three to four days.

We now know that the plague was a tiny germ, invisible except through a microscope, that lived in fleas which in turn lived on black rats. When the rats got the plague and died, the fleas moved on to humans who got the plague germ in their blood as soon as the fleas bit them. Ordinary human fleas could become infected with the plague too. Also, infected fleas could stay alive without a body to feed on for days, even weeks, as long as they were kept warm.

The fourteenth-century epidemic started in Central Asia in about 1340. From there it spread outwards towards China, India and Asia Minor where European merchants went to trade. In 1347 their ships carried infected rats back to ports in Italy and France. From there the plague spread across Europe (source 5).

activity

Look at source 5.
I How long did the Black Death take to get from Italy to Britain?
2a Make a list of all the ways in which you think the plague might be passed from place to place.
b Why do you think it usually affected towns first?

Health and medicine in the Middle Ages

It took scientists hundreds of years to understand the Black Death. It was not until 1894 that they found out what caused it. So, it is not surprising that, 500 years before, people in the Middle Ages were totally confused by the Black Death. They could not understand it and had no idea how to keep it away or cure it. They were desperate and would try anything:

SOURCE 6

Take a live frog and lay the belly of it next to the plague sore; if the patient will escape, the frog will burst in a quarter of an hour; then lay on another; and this you do till no more burst, for they draw forth the venom [poison]. If none of the frogs do burst, the person will not escape. This hath been frequently tried. Some say a dried toad will do it better.

From a book of advice on how to deal with the plague

Fourteenth-century people may not have known what to do about the plague, but they were not completely ignorant about health and disease and medicine.

activity

3 Would the cure described in source 6 have been of any use? Explain your reasons.
4a Why do you think people suggested ideas like those in source 6?
b Why do you think people tried them out?

activity

1 What evidence is there in sources 8–12 that some medieval doctors were well informed and skilful?

2 The Church did not allow people to cut open dead bodies. How does that help to explain source 7?

3 What evidence is there in sources 8 and 10 that women were important as doctors and nurses even though they were not allowed to make their living in this way?

In fact, in big households it was always someone's job, usually the lady of the house, to know how to make traditional medicines from plants and how to treat wounds. The lady of the manor often looked after people from the village if they were ill. Monks and nuns often acted as doctors in their area and sometimes ran a hospital in the monastery.

A few people actually studied to be professional doctors, often in Italy where the best medical schools were. Some of what they learnt was very useful, but some was completely mistaken. It did not help that the Church did not allow dead bodies to be opened up, so no one really knew how the human body worked:

SOURCE 7

Right in the middle of your body lies a stomach that receives whatsoever you eat or drink. This stomach is shaped like a cauldron on the fire, wherein we boil our food. You can see how if the cauldron on the fire be filled too full, then must one of two evil things come to pass. Either the cauldron must boil over or the food must burn in the cauldron . . .

A thirteenth-century doctor's description of the stomach

SOURCE 8

A chemist's shop.

Doctors also acted as surgeons; but there were not enough of them to go round so barbers (who were not trained at all) were allowed to do some simple operations such as pulling out teeth. In desperation people often went to them for other cures, but normally ended up the worse for it by being hurt or injured further.

SOURCE 10

A baby being delivered by **caesarean section**. Painted in France about 1375.

SOURCE 9

Removing an arrow. Early thirteenth century.

i John Arderne was the first well-known English surgeon. He learnt during his service in the French wars in the fourteenth century. He wrote books for the students who came to watch him.

i Caesarean section An operation to take baby from its mother's womb by making a cut in the abdomen. Doctors perform it when they think it is dangerous for a mother to give birth in the normal way.

The surgeon, **John Arderne**, wrote books for his medical students. Source 11 is the advice he gave for treating wounds, and source 12 is his advice on surgery:

SOURCE 11

Keep clean; they should heal without suppuration [forming pus]; where this occurs assist the process by washing that the wound may heal from the bottom upwards, otherwise do not dress too frequently.

John Arderne, *The Art of Medicine and Surgery*, about 1412

SOURCE 12

Drug and 'sandbag' the patient unconscious, tie up securely; if you must cut do so boldly; loss of blood is less, the shock minimised. If necessary bathe in warm water to restore temperature, put to bed, keep warm; feed well.

John Arderne, *The Art of Medicine and Surgery*, about 1412

How people behaved during the plague

SOURCE 13

This book illustration shows people burying victims of the Black Death in Tournai, Belgium.

activity

4 Look at source 5 again. Find where you live.
a Imagine you were there in 1348. Do you think you would have had any warning that the plague was approaching? Why?
b How would you have felt as you heard the news?
c What do you think you would have decided to do?

We know a little about what it must have been like during the Black Death from the writings of an Italian called Boccaccio who survived

activity

1 Look at source 15. Do you think people were right to act like this? What do you think you would have done?

the plague in Florence in 1348. Afterwards he described what happened and how people had behaved:

SOURCE 14

Most were forced by being poor to stay at home. They fell ill by the thousand and having no servants to look after them, they almost all died. Many died in the streets and the death of those at home was usually only discovered by neighbours because of the smell of their rotting corpses. Bodies lay all over the place.

Boccaccio, *Introduction to The Decameron*, 1351

SOURCE 15

Not only did citizens avoid each other, neglect their neighbours and seldom visit their relations, talking to them only from a safe distance; people were so terrified of the plague that brothers abandoned each other, uncles left nephews, wives even deserted their husbands. Worse still, and almost unheard of, parents refused to nurse and look after their own children, acting as though they were nothing to do with them.

Boccaccio, *Introduction to The Decameron*, 1351

SOURCE 16

Flagellants beating themselves.

The results of the Black Death

The Black Death had an enormous impact on the people of the Middle Ages.

Some people, called 'flagellants' (source 16), thought that the Black Death had been sent by God to punish them for their sins. They beat themselves to try to make up for their sins and to have a better chance of going to heaven when they died.

SOURCE 17

The Three Living and the Three Dead. A fourteenth-century picture.

SOURCE 18

The Dance of Death. Drawn in 1493.

SOURCE 19

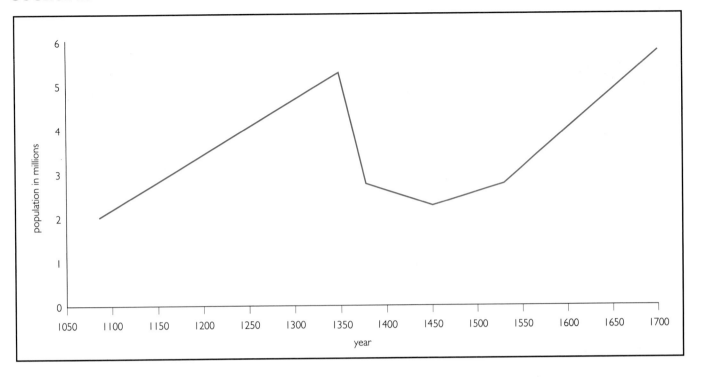

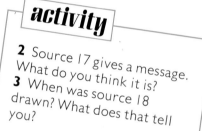

activity

2 Source 17 gives a message. What do you think it is?
3 When was source 18 drawn? What does that tell you?

So many people died in the plague epidemic that the ones who survived thought about death even more than they had before (source 17) and their fears passed on to the generations that followed.

The Black Death changed the way people lived and worked as well as how they thought. In some villages no one survived at all, in others the number of people left was sometimes as few as half the original population.

Source 19 shows you what happened to the population of Britain because of the Black Death.

The fall in population gave the lords of the manor a big problem. There were not enough peasants left to work the land and pay rent. That meant that the amount of money and food the lord received from his manor went down.

activity

4 Look at source 19.
a By how much did the population fall because of the Black Death?
b When did it get back to the level it had been in 1348, before the plague?
c How long did it take to reach this level?
d Is that what you would expect? Why?
5 If there were not so many people, there must have been fewer people to work on the same amount of land. What do you think that meant for **a** the lords, and **b** the peasants?

Some lords decided to go over to a different kind of farming that needed less people. They turned ploughland into pasture and grazed sheep on it. Sometimes they drove peasants off their land in order to do this.

Other lords decided not to ask peasants to work on the home farm any more, but asked them to pay money instead. Also they tried to put up the rent for the land the peasants held.

Most lords found that the peasants were in a strong position and that they behaved differently after the Black Death. The peasants asked for higher wages and were even prepared to bargain for them. In 1351 the landlords and merchants representing the commons in Parliament asked the king to pass a law to deal with this. It was called the *Statute of Labourers*:

SOURCE 20

a) *Against the malice [ill will] of servants who were idle and unwilling to serve after the pestilence [plague] without taking outrageous wages, it was recently ordained [ordered] by our lord the king that such servants, both men and women, should be obliged to serve in return for the salaries and wages which were customary [usual] in 1347.*

But now our lord king has been informed in this parliament, by the petition of the commons, that such servants completely disregard [ignore] the said ordinance [order] in the interest of their own ease and greed and that they withhold their service to great men and others unless they have liveries [clothing and food] and wages twice or three times as great as those they used to take.

b) *No one is to receive more than 2½d [pence] for threshing a quarter of wheat or rye. A master carpenter is to receive 3d a day; thatchers of roofs in fern and straw 3d and their boys 1¼d.*

The Statute of Labourers, 1351

The *Statute of Labourers*, however, did not have much effect:

SOURCE 21

Average daily wage rates of craftsmen and labourers.

	Thresher per quarter	Carpenter	Thatcher and helper
1331–40	2.45d	3.18d	3.82d
1341–50	2.47d	2.96d	3.73d
1351–60	4.35d	3.92d	5.00d
1361–70	4.25d	4.29d	5.95d
1371–80	4.07d	4.32d	5.98d
1381–90	3.6d	4.40d	6.01d
1391–1400	3.48d	4.13d	5.85d

activity

1a Work in a group. Read source 20 and think about it from the landlords' point of view. Why do you think they objected to demands for higher wages?
2 Now imagine that you are peasants who have heard about the *Statute of Labourers*. What arguments would you put against the statute supposing that you could get the king to listen?
3 What evidence is there in sources 21 and 22 that the Statute of Labourers did not have much effect?
4 Source 23 reports a change in the behaviour of peasants. What is it and how important do you think it was for **a** the peasants, and **b** the lords?

SOURCE 22

Walter Halderby took of divers [various] persons at reaping-time sixpence or eightpence a day, and very often at the same time made various meetings of labourers in different places and advised them not to take less.

An accusation from a court in Suffolk, late fourteenth century

SOURCE 23

As soon as their masters accuse them of bad service, or wish to pay them for their labour according to the form of the statutes, they take flight and suddenly leave their employment and district . . .

From a petition of the House of Commons, 1376

SOURCE 24

i **Hodden Grey** Hodden was the coarse woollen cloth made by country weavers. Grey hodden was undyed and so the natural colour of wool.

The world goeth from bad to worse, when shepherd and cowherd for their part demand more for their labour than the master-bailiff was wont to take in days gone by. Labourers of old were not wont to eat of wheaten bread, their meat was of beans and coarser corn, and their drink of water alone. Cheese and milk were a feast to them, and rarely ate they of other dainties; their dress was of **hodden grey**; *then was the world ordered aright for folk of this sort . . .*

John Gower, *The Mirror of Man*, 1375

assignments

I In 1363 Parliament passed a statute telling people how much they could spend, what they could wear and what possessions they could have according to their rank in society.
a Why did the king and Parliament think these things were important?
b What evidence is there in source 24 that the statute didn't make any difference?
c What evidence is there in source 24 that life was getting better for the peasants?
2a Make a list of all the consequences, or results, of the Black Death.
b Divide them into short-term consequences – things that happened at the time – and long-term consequences – things that happened later and affected people for longer.
3 There were several different kinds of consequence of the Black Death, for example:

The way people lived (Social consequences)
The wages they earned (Economic consequences)
What they thought and believed (Changes in attitudes)

Write these out as headings and find two examples to put under each.

The Peasants' Revolt

activity

1a Look at source 21. Were peasants being asked to pay more or less than an average day's pay in Poll Tax?
b The peasants said that the taxes were too high, too frequent and unfair. Do you agree?

The Poll Taxes

Peasant families were used to paying rents and services to their lord, but they were not used to being asked to pay taxes to the king. If the king needed money he usually asked the bigger landowners, such as barons or knights, and the merchants in towns to pay it. He also raised money from customs duties, especially on wool.

But in the second half of the fourteenth century, the king needed more money than usual to pay the very high cost of fighting the Hundred Years War with France. So in 1377 the government invented a new tax called a Poll Tax. 'Poll' means head. The new tax was a head-tax, a tax on each person over fifteen whoever they were and whatever they did for a living.

The government asked for the tax three times. In 1377 it asked peasants for 4d per head; in 1379 for 4d; and in 1380 for 12d. The peasants hated the tax. When officials came to collect it, they hid or lied about the number in their family. So many people managed to avoid paying that the government sent commissioners round in 1381 to find the tax-dodgers and force them to pay up.

The revolt begins

In the last week of May 1381 one of the king's tax commissioners in Essex summoned the villagers of Fobbing, Corringham and Stanford to be examined about the Poll Tax. The peasants and fishermen who lived there drove him away saying they would not pay any more taxes. Then they killed three officials sent to deal with them, stuck their heads on poles and paraded them round the neighbourhood. By June most of south Essex was up in arms.

Across the River Thames in Kent, rebels forced the king's commissioners to return to London and captured the royal castle at Rochester. Then they went to Maidstone where they chose Wat Tyler as their leader and forced the keeper of the gaol to release a priest called John Ball.

John Ball

John Ball started out as a priest in York. But the bishops did not like what he had to say so they had ordered him not to preach in church. For the past twenty years he had wandered from place to place in the south of England, preaching in the open air wherever he could find an audience.

SOURCE 25

The two main leaders of the Peasants' Revolt, painted in about 1460. Find:
- John Ball on the horse
- Wat Tyler standing on the left wearing a black hat
- the city of London in the background

What things in this picture are not likely to be true?

He told them that, if God had meant some people to be serfs and other to be lords, He would have made the world like that in the beginning. But He didn't. In the beginning He created all men equal.

Most peasants could not read but they had seen the story of Adam and Eve painted on church walls and they could remember the rhyme John Ball told them:

When Adam delved [dug] and Eve span,
Who was then the gentleman?

When the Peasants' Revolt was over, officials found that some peasants were carrying secret letters sent to them by John Ball. Source 26 is one of them:

SOURCE 26

John Ball greeteth you well and tells you to understand he had rungen your bell. Now right and might, will and skill, God speed every man. Now is the time.

activity

2 Look at source 26.
a What do you think it could mean?
b What does this tell you about John Ball's part in the revolt?

The road to London

10 June
Wat Tyler led the Kent rebels to Canterbury. They destroyed the palace of Simon Sudbury, Archbishop of Canterbury and Chancellor of England, who had helped to invent the poll tax.

11 June
The Kent rebels marched to London using the password 'King Richard and the true [loyal] Commons'. On the way they passed the king's mother returning home after a pilgrimage to Becket's shrine. No one attempted to harm her. They told the king's messenger they wanted to get rid of the 'traitors' who were advising him badly. The Essex men also moved towards London.

London

12 June
The rebels reached London. The Essex men camped at Mile End and those from Kent on Blackheath, where the leaders of both groups met. The king and his advisers took refuge in the Tower of London.

13 June
John Ball preached to the peasants on Blackheath. Then the king arrived by barge to meet the rebels at Rotherhithe. He did not land but tried to talk from the back of the barge. The peasants demanded the execution of the 'traitors' including the chancellor and the treasurer. The king and his party returned to the Tower.

A portrait of Richard II painted in 1381.

London in 1381.

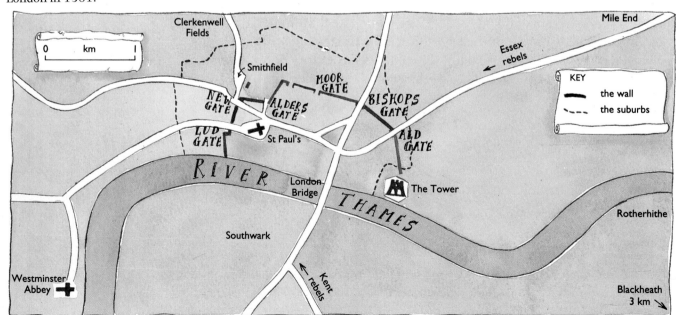

Jean Froissart (c.1337–1410) was a French poet and writer. He knew many important people and travelled widely in Western Europe collecting information for his histories. He visited England and Scotland in 1361 and returned to England in 1394–95. In his Chronicle he recorded events between 1327 and 1400, mainly from the point of view of the nobles of England and France.

SOURCE 29

Part of John Ball's sermon to the peasants at Blackheath:

Good people, things do not go well in England, nor will they until everyone is equal and there are neither villeins nor gentlemen, and lords be no greater than we are . . .

They are dressed in velvet, while we have to wear poor cloth. They have wines, spices and fine bread, while we have to make do with coarse bread and water. They have the fine houses while we must face the pain of working in the wind and rain in the fields.

Let us go to the king, he is young, and show him what slavery we are in. Let us tell him that we want things to be put right or else we will do something about it ourselves.

Jean Froissart *Chronicle*, completed about 1401

Angry peasants entered London and surrounded the Tower of London. They demanded to see the king who agreed to meet them next morning outside the city at Mile End.

activity

1a What evidence is there in source 29 that the peasants thought of the king as their friend not their enemy?
b What other evidence to support this is there in the events of 10–13 June?
c What does John Ball say will happen if the king will not help?
d Do you think the peasants would have described themselves as 'rebels'? Explain your answer.
2 What do you think the effect of John Ball's speech would have been on:
a the peasants who heard it;
b the lords who had the words reported to them?
3 Jean Froissart was not on Blackheath to hear John Ball preach. How much should we trust this source?
4 Imagine you are one of Richard II's advisers in the Tower of London on the evening of 13 June. The king has very few soldiers in London. What would you advise him to do?

14 June

The king rode out to Mile End with a small escort. Wat Tyler then asked the king to grant that:

- serfdom should be abolished
- labour services should be abolished and landholders should pay a low fixed rent
- everyone who had taken part in the rebellion should be given a free pardon
- the king's advisers should be punished

The king agreed to have charters written to grant all these demands except the last. Most of the Essex men went off home, but those from Kent were still not satisfied. Some of them went to the Tower and dragged out the chancellor, the treasurer and two others and executed them. That evening there were riots in London. The king invited the rebels to meet him again the next afternoon at Smithfield.

15 June

When the king arrived at Smithfield with 200 followers to meet several thousand peasants, Wat Tyler rode over, greeted the king and made further demands.

Then someone shouted, 'This man is the greatest robber and thief in Kent.' Tyler drew his dagger and in the scuffle that followed a royal attendant ran him through with his sword. Tyler managed to turn his horse and ride a little way back across the field. Then he fell to the ground half-dead. There was a cry of fury from the peasants

activity

1 What evidence is there from the events of 10–14 June that the peasants wanted to get revenge on particular people? Who were these people and what had they done?

2 You are one of the king's advisers on the evening of 14 June. What would you advise him to do when he meets the peasants at Smithfield the next day?

SOURCE 30

Painted about 1460, this shows two events in one picture.
On the left the Mayor of London is about to strike Wat Tyler with his sword, while the king looks on.
On the right Richard II rides over to talk to the rebels.

and they drew back their bows to shoot. The king and his followers were an arrow-flight from death.

At that moment Richard rode forward to the peasants and called:

SOURCE 31

Sirs, will you shoot your king? I will be your chief and captain, you shall have from me that which you seek. Only follow me into the fields without.

Jean Froissart, *Chronicle*

The king rode north towards Clerkenwell fields. After a moment's hesitation the peasants followed him.

The Mayor of London gathered a well-armed force of 1,000 men. He found the dying Wat Tyler and had him executed. Then, with Tyler's head on a pole, he rode out to the king, who was surrounded by peasants but unharmed.

Seeing that their leader was dead and they were now faced by determined troops, the peasants agreed to the king's command to go home. He refused to have any one else executed and ordered that the charters promised at Mile End should still be given to them.

The end of the revolt

As the peasants set off home, the king started to break his promises. First he forced every Londoner to swear an oath of loyalty. Then he led his army out to Essex. There he told peasants who asked him to keep the promises he had made at Mile End:

SOURCE 32

Oh you wretched men, detestable on land and sea, give this message to your companions: 'Villeins you are still, and villiens you shall remain.'

From the writings of Thomas Walsingham, 1381

The peasants' leaders were hunted out and hanged. At the beginning of July the king announced that on the advice of his council he was taking back all his grants of freedom and pardon because he made them 'in haste to the rebels'. John Ball was caught in the Midlands and hanged on 15 July.

The results of the revolt

In the end the king and the lords crushed the Peasants' Revolt: but it certainly frightened them. The king never again tried to use a Poll Tax to raise money. For a few years Parliament carried on trying to keep wages down but then it gave up. The peasants did not all get their freedom as they wanted in 1381. But there were still not

SOURCE 33

A peasant hanging.

enough peasants to work the land, so lords gradually gave up trying to make them give labour services. By 1500 there were no villeins.

activity

1 Look at source 34. What do you think these punishments meant to the families of each of these men?

SOURCE 34

William Guildeborn:	hanged, 5th July; his goods seized, among them 75 sheep
Thomas Guildeborn:	a fugitive.
Richard Frannceys:	hanged, his goods seized, among them a cottage
John Wolk:	hanged, his goods seized.
John Devin:	his goods seized
Ralph White:	his goods seized
Ralph Tripat:	a fugitive
Robert Knight:	a fugitive; his goods seized, among them a boat with all its gear (oars, sails etc.)

The record of punishments given to the men of Fobbing.

assignments

1 Of all the sources 25–34 which we have used for the Peasants' Revolt only one was written by someone on the peasants' side.
a Which one is it?
All the others come from writers or artists who were sympathetic to the king and the lords, though sometimes they report what the peasants' leaders are supposed to have said.
b Why do you think we have so few sources from the peasants?
c What difference do you think it would make if we had more?

2 It is often useful to divide the causes of an event into two kinds. The 'long-term' causes are the ones that have been going on for a long time and make the event possible. The 'short-term', or 'immediate' causes, are the ones that come just before the event and set it off. For example, when a tree comes down in a storm, the short-term cause is the storm. The long-term cause is whatever makes it likely that the tree will fall in a high wind. Perhaps it has rotted inside, or its roots are weak, or it has grown too tall.
a Here are two long-term and two short-term causes of the Peasants' Revolt. Add as many others as you can to each list.

Long-term causes
● Peasants lived hard lives in very bad conditions.
● The Black Death killed many peasants so there was a shortage of labour.

Short-term causes
● The king needed money to fight the French Wars.
● Wat Tyler was a strong leader.

b Decide which you think are the two most important of (i) the long-term and (ii) the short-term causes and give the reasons for your choice.

3 Look again at what Wat Tyler told Richard II in source 2. Which do you think did more in the end to win the peasants their freedom, the Black Death or the Peasants' Revolt? Why?

The invention of the printing press

Sometime around 1450 a new invention appeared in the town of Mainz in Germany. It was a machine called a 'printing press' and it could be used to print books instead of writing them out by hand. The printing press changed peoples' lives more than any other invention in the Middle Ages.

Source 1 shows how books were made before the invention of printing. The monk is writing or copying a book by hand and is writing on a scroll of parchment. Parchment is made from sheepskin. A 150-page book used up the skins of 12 sheep. Sheep skins cost a lot of money because sheep were more use alive than dead. Why do you think that was?

The inventor of the Mainz printing press was a goldsmith called Johannes Gutenberg who used his metal-working skills to devise a way of making metal **type** in moulds.

Source 2 shows an early printing press being used. The two men at the back keep pieces of metal type in slots in the sloping trays in

activity

1 How are the books stored in source1?

2 Make a list of the reasons why **a** there were not many copies of each book before the invention of the printing press, and **b** books made in this way were expensive.

3 Paper was much cheaper than parchment so printed books were cheaper than hand-written copies. What other differences do you think the printing press made?

SOURCE 1

Making a book by hand.

SOURCE 2

An early printing press.

> **ℹ Type** Gutenburg wasn't the first person to use lots of separate pieces of moveable type that could be made up into words. The Chinese had been doing this from about 1040. They first tried making their type out of pottery and then tin, but these were too soft and breakable. By the fourteenth century they were using wood, and in the fifteenth century they started to use metal.

> **ℹ Paper** If it had not been for the Chinese there would have been no paper in Europe to print on. The Chinese had invented paper making in the second century AD. Their method had gradually been passed west along the trade routes. It reached southern Spain in the twelfth century and from there it slowly moved into the rest of Europe. In the fourteenth century there were factories in Italy and France making paper from rags.

front of them. Each piece will print a letter of the alphabet and they are put together in a box called a 'forme' to make the words of the book to be printed. The man on the right is holding a forme. A group of formes are put together to make up a page.

The printer at the front on the right is holding an ink pad in each hand. His job is to ink the metal type before pressing the **paper** down on it. He is inking the formes that make up two pages of the book. Beside him is the press.

William Caxton

Gutenberg's invention was spread rapidly round Europe by printing workers who moved about looking for places to set up business. It reached England in 1476 when William Caxton set up a printing business in Westminster just outside the city of London.

Caxton was not a printing worker. He was a successful merchant who had spent many years living and working in the port of Bruges, in modern Belgium, trading mainly in wool and cloth and sometimes in illuminated manuscripts.

In 1471 he left Bruges to go to Cologne and there he learnt how printing was done. Then he returned to Bruges, where he translated books from French into English, had them printed on his own press and shipped them to England. Four years later he returned home and set up in Westminster.

SOURCE 3

A page from the *Game of Chess*, the second book ever to be printed in English. William Caxton translated the book from French into English and printed it in Bruges in 1474.

SOURCE 4

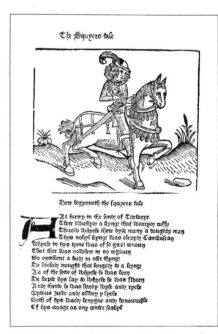

The title page of *The Squire's Tale* in the second edition of Chaucer's *Canterbury Tales*, printed by Caxton in Westminster in about 1483.

The English language

Up until the middle of the fourteenth century, Latin and French were the languages used for government and by the upper classes. However things began to change:

- in 1362 English was made the language of the law courts instead of French
- in 1363 the chancellor spoke for the first time in English instead of Latin when he opened Parliament
- from 1370 onwards Geoffrey Chaucer was writing his poetry in English
- the earliest known will to be written in English dates from 1387
- in 1399 Henry, Duke of Lancaster, spoke in English instead of French when he formally claimed the throne

The effects of printing

You can get some idea of the effects of printing in the fifteenth and sixteenth centuries if you think about the way television has changed peoples' lives in the twentieth century.

SOURCE 5

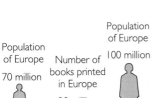
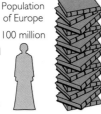

Population of Europe
70 million

Number of books printed in Europe
20 million

Population of Europe
100 million

Number of books printed in Europe
175 million

1450 - 1500

1500 - 1600

activity

1 Look at source 6. What difference do you think the invention of printing made to the people shown there?

2 Source 7 shows part of the first ever translation of the Bible into English. Was it printed or written by hand?

3 In 1526 William Tyndale finished translating his version of the Bible into English. It was printed.

a Why do you think he wanted it to be printed?

b The Church opposed the idea of people reading a translation of the Bible. Why do you think this was?

c What do you think the Church thought about printing translations of the Bible?

SOURCE 6

Students listening to an open-air lecture at New College, Oxford, in 1463. Many schools were founded in the fifteenth century. The universities of Oxford and Cambridge, which had started in the late twelfth and early thirteenth centuries, grew larger. New universities were founded in Scotland at St Andrews, Glasgow and Aberdeen.

SOURCE 7

A page from John Wyclif's English translation of the Bible. In 1382 John Wyclif translated the Bible into English for the first time. He believed that some teachings of the Church were wrong and that the Bible said what was right. He wanted everyone to have a copy of the Bible in English.

assignments

1a How did life change as a result of the invention of printing?

b Whose life changed the most? Whose changed the least?

c How quickly do you think the changes happened?

d Who benefited from printing?

2 Some changes mean that people do things differently. Some changes make life worse; some make life better. When things improve we call this 'progress'.

a The effect of the change from writing books by hand to printing them is usually described as progress. Why do you think this is?

b You have read about many things that changed in this book: (i) find another change in the Middle Ages which led to progress; (ii) find a change which did not lead to progress.

3 Which of these inventions do you think caused the greatest change: the printing press; the telephone; the typewriter; the television; the computer? Use the library to help you find out about each one. Then either write an article or give a talk to explain what you think and why.

In August 1485, two English armies confronted each other at Bosworth Field in Leicestershire. One was led by the king, Richard III; the other by Henry Tudor, Earl of Richmond. Two hours later the king's army was defeated, Richard himself was dead and his crown lay in a thorn bush where it had dropped as he fell. Lord Stanley picked it up and placed it on the victor's head. Henry Tudor had become Henry VII, King of England.

Henry VII was the third king to seize the crown by force since 1461 and no one in 1485 could be sure he would be the last. As it turned out, he was. The Battle of Bosworth Field ended thirty years of civil wars that have come to be known as the 'Wars of the Roses'.

The wars were a struggle for the throne of England between the two great families of York and Lancaster. They were first called the 'Wars of the Roses' in a *History of England* published in 1762. This was because the red rose was the emblem of the Lancaster family and the white rose was the emblem of the York family.

At the time of the wars, people had no special name for them. It was Henry VII who made the roses important. In 1486 he married Edward IV's daughter, Elizabeth, and so united the two families of York and Lancaster. To show that he had done this and that he stood for a united peaceful country he combined the red and white roses into a double rose (source 1) which became the emblem of the Tudors.

SOURCE 1

Henry VII's double rose in a stained-glass window.

Opinions about the fifteenth century

Tudor kings and queens ruled until 1603. During that time every history of the fifteenth century described it as a time of terrible wars and bloodshed, of violence and disorder. In the nineteenth century, historians still took the same view. Bishop Stubbs described the fifteenth century as a time of 'clouds and darkness' and he said:

SOURCE 2

The most enthusiastic admirer of medieval life must grant [agree] that all that was good and great in it was languishing [growing weak] even to death – and the firmest believer in progress must admit there were few signs of returning health.

Bishop Stubbs, *Constitutional History of England*, 1878

Kings and wars in the fifteenth century

Richard II

Richard was only ten when he came to the throne so a council helped him to rule; but the most important person was John of Gaunt, Duke of Lancaster. After his success against the peasants in 1381, Richard faced increasing opposition from the barons, especially John of Gaunt's son, Henry Bolingbroke, Duke of Hereford. Eventually, Bolingbroke, supported by some barons, captured the king and forced him to give up the throne in favour of Bolingbroke who became King Henry IV. Richard died in 1400 in Henry's castle at Pontefract, probably murdered though there is no proof.

Henry IV

Henry had a weak title to the throne even though Parliament had accepted him. This was to be a problem later for the Lancastrians. It was a good thing that he was an excellent soldier as he spent much of his reign dealing with rebellions.

Battle of Agincourt

| | RICHARD II | HENRY IV | HENRY V | |
|1370|1380|1390|1400|1410|1420|1430|

Henry V

Henry IV's son and a brilliant general, Henry V re-opened the Hundred Years War by claiming the throne of France. He defeated a far larger French army at the famous Battle of Agincourt and by 1420 he had conquered Normandy, married the French king's daughter and had persuaded the French king to name him as his successor. But in 1422 he fell ill and died, aged 35.

Henry VI

Henry was only nine months old when his father, Henry V, died and he became king. He was crowned King of France in Paris in 1431 but by 1453 the French had driven the English out of the whole of France except Calais. Henry liked books, paintings, peace and quiet. In 1453 he was proclaimed mad and the Duke of York acted as Regent. York wanted the crown himself and a civil war began. In 1459 York publicly claimed the throne. After York's death in battle in 1461, his son captured London and proclaimed himself King Edward IV. Henry was his prisoner for all but a year (1470–71) when he was briefly

Edward IV

Edward IV strengthened his position as king by defeating the Lancastrians at the Battle of Towton in 1461. But he later quarrelled with Warwick, his strongest supporter, who then changed sides and managed to restore Henry VI to the throne in 1470. After victories at Barnet and Tewkesbury in 1471, Edward ruled for the next twelve years without challenge and in that time managed to restore the power of the king's government throughout the realm.

Richard III

Richard, Duke of Gloucester, had himself crowned in July 1483, claiming the throne as a younger brother of Edward IV. He was a good soldier and strong ruler. However, many people disliked the way he had treated Edward V and there were rumours that Richard had had Edward and his brother murdered. Many historians today think that the evidence for this was invented by Henry VII.

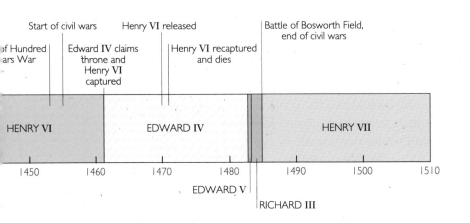

	Start of civil wars		Henry VI released		Battle of Bosworth Field, end of civil wars	
of Hundred ars War	Edward IV claims throne and Henry VI captured		Henry VI recaptured and dies			
HENRY VI		EDWARD IV			HENRY VII	
1450	1460	1470	1480	1490	1500	1510

EDWARD V

RICHARD III

restored to the throne by the Earl of Warwick who acted as the real ruler. In 1471, Edward recaptured Henry who died, probably murdered, shortly afterwards in the Tower of London.

Edward V

Edward V succeeded his father in 1483, aged thirteen. His uncle, Richard, Duke of Gloucester, declared himself Protector and had Edward and his younger brother imprisoned in the Tower of London. They disappeared and were probably murdered.

Henry VII

Henry Tudor, Earl of Richmond, had become head of the Lancastrian family when Henry VI died. People opposed to Richard III went to join him in France where he planned his invasion. After his victory over Richard at Bosworth in 1485, Henry ruled until his death in 1509. He married Edward IV's daughter, Elizabeth, so uniting the houses of York and Lancaster.

The Tudor view of the fifteenth century

In 1548 a new book came off the printing presses. It was a chronicle by Edward Hall and it was called 'The Union of two noble and illustrious families of Lancaster and York, being long in continual dissension [disagreement] for the crown of this noble realm . . . beginning at the time of King Henry IV, the first author of this division'. There was no doubt about Hall's point of view:

SOURCE 3

What misery, what murder and what execrable [detestable] plagues this famous country hath suffered by the division and dissension of the renowned houses of Lancaster and York, my wit cannot comprehend [understand] nor my tongue declare, neither yet my pen fully set forth.

Edward Hall, *The Union*, 1548

Later in the sixteenth century, William Shakespeare wrote eight plays about the events of the fifteenth century and he used Edward Hall's chronicle as his source for what happened. Like Hall he tried to show how terrible the civil wars had been.

Shakespeare did not always show actual historical events in his plays. In *Henry IV, Part I* he invented a famous scene in a garden in which the quarrelling barons picked red and white roses to show which side they were on. Source 4 shows a nineteenth-century picture of this scene.

SOURCE 4

Choosing the red and white roses. Painted by Henry A. Payne (1868–1939). Several nineteenth-century artists painted this scene.

activity

I Look at the information about kings and wars on pages 122–23. How does it support Hall's view of the fifteenth century?

activity

2 Look at source 4.
a Is this evidence that people in later times were influenced by Shakespeare's view of the fifteenth century?
b Why do you think artists liked to paint this particular scene?
c Did pictures like this give an accurate view of the events of the fifteenth century?

i **Philippe de Commynes** was a French politician who lived from 1447 to 1511. He was an adviser first to the duke of Burgundy and then to the king of France. He travelled on missions to Spain and Italy as well as England.

Another sixteenth-century writer, Sir Thomas More, also wrote a history of the last years of the Wars of the Roses:

SOURCE 5

Richard was evil and full of anger and envy. He was secretive and could hide his real feelings. He looked very humble but he was really very arrogant, pretending to like people he wanted to kill. He was cruel and pitiless, not always because he was evil, but sometimes because he was ambitious and wanted more power.

Sir Thomas More, *History of King Richard III*, 1513

Another point of view

The Tudor idea that the fifteenth century in general and the Wars of the Roses in particular were a time of darkness and gloom was accepted by historians in the nineteenth century (source 2) and even went on into the twentieth century. Most historians today think that this view is wrong. Use the sources and information on the following pages to work out why.

Some information about the Wars of the Roses:

Number of weeks of active military campaigning between 1455 and 1487: **about 52**

Number of weeks of actual fighting 1455–87: **about 13**

Estimated numbers involved in battles:

St Albans (1455) **5,000**	Barnet (1471) **24,000**
Towton (1461) **50,000**	Bosworth Field (1485) **20–25,000**

Number of nobles killed, murdered or executed 1455–85: Kings **3**; Prince of Wales **1**; Dukes **9**; Marquis **1**; Earls **13**; Barons **24**

SOURCE 6

Towton . . . involved the largest armies of the war. One chronicler's . . . estimate of 9,000 dead – 10% of the combatants – is likely to be near the mark. Even this rate of casualties was probably quite exceptional. In most battles the dead were probably to be numbered in hundreds rather than thousands.

C. Ross, *The Wars of the Roses*, 1976

SOURCE 7

Out of all the countries which I have personally known, England is the one where public affairs are best conducted and regulated with least violence to the people. There neither the countryside nor the people are destroyed, nor are buildings burnt or demolished. Disaster and misfortune fall only on those who make war, the soldiers and the nobles.

Philippe de Commynes, *Memoirs*, c.1500

activity

3 Later in life, after he had written source 5, Sir Thomas More quarrelled with King Henry VIII. The king ordered that all Sir Thomas More's books which he did not agree with should no longer be printed. But he allowed his *History of King Richard III* to be reprinted four times.
a What picture of Richard does Sir Thomas More give in source 5?
b Why do you think Henry VIII did not ban this book too?
c If the Tudors had not liked Edward Hall's book they could have stopped it being printed. Why do you think they did like it?

activity

4 Look at the information opposite and sources 6 and 7.
a Which of these is a primary source and which is a secondary source?
b What evidence is there that:
(i) The civil wars probably did not affect many ordinary people?
(ii) The wars were probably most damaging to the barons?
(iii) Casualties were not particularly high?
(iv) Fewer people were killed than were usual because the wars were civil wars?
(v) The wars did not really go on continually for thirty years?
c How reliable do you think the evidence of Philippe de Commynes is likely to be and why?

SOURCE 8

The West gate at Canterbury.

SOURCE 9

The South gate at King's Lynn.

SOURCE 10

Town councils had walls built and kept in repair so that the town could defend itself against attack. Towns had to ask the king for permission to raise special taxes to pay for this. The number of towns that did this in the thirteenth, fourteenth and fifteenth centuries were:

13th century	14th century	15th century
1260: 14	1360: 7	1460: 9
1270: 17	1370: 17	1470: 9
1280: 10	1380: 15	1480: 6
1290: 10	1390: 15	1490: 4

activity

I Look at sources 8 and 9. One town gate was designed for defence and was built in the fourteenth century. The other is much wider and was designed as a toll gate for carts to pass through. It was built in the fifteenth century.
a Which is which?
b Does that support the 'dark and gloomy' view of the fifteenth century or not?

2 Look at source 10.
a In which century were towns most conerned to raise money to build and repair walls, and in which were they least concerned?
b What does this tell you about the fifteenth century?

SOURCE 11

Tattershall Castle, Lincolnshire.

activity

3 Lord Cromwell built Tattershall Castle (source 11) in the second half of the fifteenth century.
a What evidence is there that it was more of a house than a castle?
b Why would it be of little use against guns?
c Does it suggest Lord Cromwell thought that he might need to defend himself?

SOURCE 12

The church tower at Evercreech, Somerset. This was one of many churches built in the fifteenth century in the 'Perpendicular' style, often paid for by rich wool merchants.

SOURCE 13

The chapel of King's College, Cambridge. It was started in the reign of Henry VI and finished in the reign of Henry VIII.

activity

4 What do sources 12 and 13 tell you about:
a the skills of English stonemasons in the fifteenth century?
b the wealth of England at that time?
5 What other evidence is there in Part 4, and Part 9 that many people in fifteenth-century England were prosperous and creative?

assignments

1a Use the sources and information on pages 124–25 to make a list of the various criticisms that Tudor historians made of the fifteenth century.
b How do the sources and information on pages 125–27 show that the Tudors were wrong about the fifteenth century?

2a If you only had the information on pages 122 and 123, what view of life in the fifteenth century would it give you?
b Would the sources on pages 124–25 change that view or not?
c What does this tell you about how important it is to look at as many different sources as possible and compare them?

Overview

1 Imagine that you are an adviser to Henry VIII in 1485. The new king asks you: **a** to tell him as much as you can about the kingdom of England, and **b** to recommend what needs to be done now that he is king. Write the report that you would give him.

2 You have found out about many different types of people in the Middle Ages. Here are some of them: kings, barons, priests, peasants, townspeople. Choose any three of these.
a How did things change for each of them during the Middle Ages?
b In what ways did things stay the same?

3 Women made up about half the population in the Middle Ages, but it is very difficult to find out what their lives were like.
a How many sources in this book are either by women or about women?
b What can we tell about the lives of women from these sources?
c Does the fact that there are so few sources written by women mean that they did very little?

4 Many of the sources in this book are things made by artists and craftspeople, for example, buildings, illuminated manuscripts, stained-glass windows, and paintings.
a Can you see any differences between things made around 1100 and things made around 1500?
b Do you think artists and craftspeople became more skilful during the Middle Ages?
c Do you think they were more skilful than artists and craftspeople today?

5 The kingdom of England was part of a wider world throughout the Middle Ages. It was linked to other places by: kings and barons, trade, the church, learning. Choose two of these.
a What were the links in each case in (i) 1100, and (ii) 1500?
b Do you think England's links with the wider world were greater in 1500 than in 1100?